i

Tekakwitha: Holy Native, Mohawk Virgin 1656-1680

"I will love you in heaven; I will help you; I will pray for you."

Catherine "Kateri" Tekakwitha

Tekakwitha: Holy Native, Mohawk Virgin 1656-1680

By Rev. Edward Sherman, Compiler/Author of Life Story,
with Reflections

Fine Print of Grand Forks, Inc.   Grand Forks, ND 58201

I dedicate this book to my mother, my father, and my sister. I only wish I had appreciated them even more, asked them more questions, or at least listened better. I feel the same about Tekakwitha, and her father, mother, and all relatives.

Rev. Edward Sherman

The horizontal emblem appearing on the cover just to the left of Tekakwitha is the emblem adopted by the Iroquois nations. Centuries ago they formed a confederation, and depicted themselves gathered in unity about the tree of unity.

This book has been printed by Fine Print of Grand Forks, ND,
but it is not available through them. To obtain a copy,
contact Cardinal Muench Seminary,
100 35th Avenue NE, Fargo, ND 58102-1299.
Telephone (701) 232-8969 or e-mail: b.hagemeier@cardinalmuench.org.

The cost per book is $12.00 (U.S.) plus postage and handling
($3.50 for the first book and $1.00 for each additional book).

Make your check or money order payable to: Cardinal Muench Seminary

ISBN 978-0-9796390-0-5

2nd Printing
Printed U.S.A.

Contents

Introduction

Catherine "Kateri" Tekakwitha, an American Indian, lived in a time that may seem long ago. But from the very day of her death in 1680 many people have almost felt her presence, and reverently longed to know more about her. That reverence for her has brought her the title "Blessed." It seems certain that someday—hopefully soon—the Catholic Church will officially bestow on her the title she deserves; that is, to be addressed as "Saint." With good reason we write about her.

Tekakwitha's life story and what has happened since her time will attest that she is now in heaven, a saint in the fullest sense. But before that full official recognition comes, this author wonders just what will be said about her—and about her family and people—when it does come.

The presentation of details about Tekakwitha's life is certainly needed. Skeptics may arise, but they must not be able to argue that she should not have been described as a saint.

Along with describing and knowing the details of her life before she went to heaven, perhaps it is even more important to highlight the benefit her life and death gives to us who still remain in this world. To say that she was and is a saint is not nearly as helpful as an effort to say and to know what her Christian life means for us in our present pursuit. What is there about her that is so holy, so appealing, and so helpful?

This text presents only a little of what can be said, but hopefully it will be a small help in making Catherine better known to present-day people. And it is a venerable Catholic view that our knowledge of God is enhanced by knowing God's holy people. "Blessed be God in His angels and in His saints!"

Unfortunately there might be confusion about this particular holy person's name, and this could make people discouraged in following the story of her life. Her Native name was Tekakwitha, but at Baptism she went under the patronage of St. Catherine, and took the name of that holy fourteenth-century virgin. Though some early versions or translations spell her name Katharine, this text will almost always call her Catherine. Admittedly most people have come to know her as Kateri, and this is probably because of the way Mohawk speakers pronounced her name. Fairly recently, some English speakers deferred to this, and began calling her Kateri.

It must be kept in mind that the Catholic Church will officially list a person as a saint only when a clear and fairly recent physical miracle is received from God through that holy one's special intercession. With the encouragement of the Church, many pray continually for such a miracle. With that in mind, a special prayer is printed toward the end of this book.

Acknowledgements

There are numerous articles and books which can introduce the reader to the life of Blessed Catherine "Kateri" Tekakwitha. Their stories and explanations tell about the venerable Native American woman who lived from 1656 to 1680.

Most important is *The Positio of the Historical Section of the Sacred Congregation of Rites on the Introduction of the Cause for the Beatification and Canonization and on the Virtues of the Servant of God Catherine Tekakwitha, the Lily of the Mohawks.* It is the Catholic Church's anthology of writings "placed as evidence" of Catherine's holiness and worthiness of the public titles of "Blessed" and "Saint." An English translation of this *Positio* was published by Fordham University Press in 1940 and 2002. Though libraries make it possible to read these early writings, Monsignor Paul A. Lenz's gift of a personal copy has been a wonderful help to this author in his study of Tekakwitha's life.

The materials in the *Positio*, classified there as "Documents," were written over several decades beginning in 1682 by French missionaries. Excerpts will appear throughout this volume, and their location in the 1940 Fordham Press edition will be indicated. Permission for their use has been sought from that publisher. Most of the *Positio* quotes are from two men: Father Chauchetière (1645-1709) and Father Cholenec (1640-1723).

A list of the recent century's writings would include: *Glory of the Mohawks* by Edward LeCompte, S.J. (1926, 1944); *Catherine Tekakwitha* by Daniel Sargent (1940); *Kateri of the Mohawks* by Marie Cecilia Buehrle (1954); *Kateri Tekakwitha* by F.X. Weiser, S.J. (1971); *Mystic of the Wilderness* by Margaret Bunson (1992); "The Making of the First Iroquois Virgin" by K.J. Koppedrayer (Spring 1993); *Kateri Tekakwitha* by Henry Béchard, S.J. (1994); "Tekakwitha" by (Sister) Marie Therese Archambault OSF (1996), and others. Perhaps most recent, and of special value, is *Mohawk Saint: Catherine Tekakwitha and the Jesuits* by Allan Greer of the University of Toronto (2005). Professor Greer describes the surroundings and the aftermath of Catherine's life, and the background and mentality of those who knew her and wrote about her. *The Iroquois* by Dean R. Snow (1994, 1996), was also an immense help.

Reverend William Sherman, Doctor Leigh Jeanotte and his staff at the American Indian Center at the University of North Dakota, and many others who also deserve thanks, have helped greatly.

Appreciation is extended to Monsignor Lenz for the above mentioned gift, and for his encouragement to complete this work. And the Tekakwitha Conference, whose headquarters is in Great Falls, MT, and Director Sister Kateri Mitchell, are completely dedicated to making Tekakwitha known. It is evident that in their very effective work of uplifting Catherine "Kateri" Tekakwitha, they are uplifting present-day people, and are helping very many to uplift one another.

Professor Allan Greer and Sister Archambault, rightly-recognized scholars, sent kind responses to my inquiries, and those have been both helpful and very encouraging.

The majority of drawings reproduced herein are from Fordham University Press publications; permission has been asked for their use. Other copyrighted materials are noted with each entry, and permission to use any and all of these has been sought.

Courtesy of Fordham University Press, from their *Positio*. Permission received.

A baby is cared for by a loving and hard-working parent. The story in this text will show what wonderful things came from loving parents and their daughter, Catherine "Kateri" Tekakwitha.

Chapter One: The Iroquoian People and the Coming of the Europeans.

Courtesy of the Fordham University Press, from their *Positio*. Permission received.

Many duties filled the days of the Mohawks, Catherine Tekakwitha's people.

This story centers about a young American Indian, a member of the Mohawk people. That people are part of the Iroquoian Confederation, called the "People of the Longhouse," a name they received from the lodgings they constructed. Such lodges, which by our standards may seem primitive, provided them with a surprising degree of comfort. They were clustered into villages—which some have called castles surrounded by wooden palisades—all of which was the product of a thousand years of experience.[1] From their lodges, they hunted and cultivated fields not far from the Atlantic coast.

Photo by E. Sherman

The river called the Mohawk runs near villages built by people most often called the Mohawk people. It is in the east central part of the present-day State of New York, and flows into the Hudson River about 160 miles north of New York City.

The Mohawks are the most easterly of the Iroquoian people, and even today they call themselves "The Keepers of the Eastern Gate." Their neighbors, from east to west, are the Oneidas, Onondagas, Cayugas,

---

[1] Dean R. Snow, *Iroquois*, Blackwell, Oxford, UK, 1994, 1996, p.27.

and Senecas. This total of five nations formed a confederation sometime before 1525. In 1712, a sixth nation, the Tuscarora, was welcomed and added to the confederation.

Courtesy of Kateri Shrine and Indian Museum, Fonda, NY, from the shrine's brochure.

Longhouses (also called bark houses) were constructed by the Mohawk people, and sheeted with elm bark. Many were divided into sections, one for each family, and several in each house. The house style was also used by the other Iroquoians.

By the mid-1600s Europeans had been setting foot on the continent for over a hundred years.

Samuel Champlain Stamp Design copyright 2006 United States Postal Service. All Rights Reserved. Used with permission.

Many non-Natives arrived from across the ocean in sailing ships that at first awed Native people. Vikings are said to have come earlier, but Christopher Columbus of course came in 1492. To the Canadian areas, Jacques Cartier first came in 1534. Samuel de Champlain, whose voyage is commemorated above, was with another arriving group as early as 1603. Christian missionaries also came from Europe in those earliest years.

This text cannot deal adequately with the cultural destruction done to the Mohawks and other Native peoples by the coming of the Europeans. That harm, by any standards, was dreadful! It is hard to realize that a blessing needed to come at such a cost. Yet for numbers of Native people, in spite of the many terrible events, there is something they consider a blessing: it is the ability to know the good news of and about Jesus Christ. This text will focus on the faith in Jesus Christ that many Native people embrace, and how one group in particular became fully Catholic Christian.

Courtesy *The European Challenge*

The new continent turned out to be vast. In describing it, and its people, newcomers used different words, such as "wilderness" or even "savage." Because words often carry the attitude of the user, a study of words or names can be very helpful. One such word that turns up in English is the word "savage." The above picture may, for some, look "savage." Later in this text a discussion of such a term is presented. Some very unfortunate meanings are sometimes conveyed when the original meaning of that term is not known.

A Mohawk village that has come to be known as Ossernenon,[2] was near the Mohawk River some 30 miles west of the Hudson River in present-day New York. That village, which is remembered at a well-kept

---

[2] The village name *Ossernenon* appears in some writings such as those of Father Isaac Jogues, whose martyrdom took place, and is now commemorated in that locality. The approximate location of his death is now known as the National Shrine of the North American Martyrs. It is near Auriesville, NY. The village there is called by the name *Ossernenon*, though some authorities refer to it as *Gandaouagué*.

modern shrine, is an important beginning to this story, for it is said to be the birthplace of Tekakwitha. A picture of a marker at the Ossernenon village is below.

Photo by E. Sherman at Shrine of North American Martyrs, Auriesville. NY

The National Shrine of the North American Martyrs at Auriesville, NY, offers an opportunity to ponder not only several martyrdoms but, just a few years later, a wonderful birth.

Mohawks, as did other Iroquoian people, had their "home" villages, but frequently they went north to the St. Lawrence River. From those ventures, which were often violent, they brought back men and women from the Algonquian peoples. Some women would become wives to Iroquois men.

Courtesy of St. Francis Xavier Church/Museum, Kahnawake, Canada

This statue portrays a typical Native wife and mother at work. The sculptor no doubt had in mind a woman who originally was from the Algonquian people in Canada, and who became the wife of a Mohawk chieftain.

Some time in the mid-seventeenth century, Mohawk warriors or hunters brought back to their village an Indian woman whose name does not seem to have been recorded.[3] It is known that she had been baptized and raised as a Catholic near Three Rivers in Canada. Some authors refer to her as "Kahenta." In her new place, she was married to a Mohawk man and the new family lived in the village near present-day Auriesville, New York. Their first child was a girl.

Before long the couple had two children. Sadly however, their family life was interrupted by the coming of the scourge of smallpox. The ones who were the actual carriers of that disease may possibly have been the children of nearby Dutch settlers, who had the nearby Fort Orange (now Albany, New York.)[4]

Courtesy of Dean R. Snow, in *The Iroquois*

Fort Orange, as in a 1630 painting by L. F. Tantillo, was settled by Dutch people,
and was near where the Mohawk River Flows into the Hudson River.

---

3 Father Claude Chauchetière, *La Vie de la B. Catherine Tegakoüita dite à present La Sainte Saugavesse, (Positio* Document VIII 1685, 1695, p. 120.) (hereafter called *Op.Cit.*)

4 Snow, *Op.Cit.*, p. 99.

The smallpox epidemic killed the young mother and the younger child, a boy. It likely also caused the death of the father, for the older child—the girl now just a few years old—was thereafter cared for by relatives.

Courtesy of Monastery Immaculate Conception, Ferdinand, IN

Above is a painting by a more recent American Indian parent wanting to remember the beauty of a daughter.

The girl, this book's subject, also suffered the terrible disease. It left her poor little face scarred terribly, and her eyes very weak. Her name is known for certain: it is "Tekakwitha" (Te-ka-KWEE-tha). She later, as a Christian, was named after Saint Catherine of Siena, a holy, very influential, fourteen-century Italian virgin. This text could always speak of her as "Tekakwitha," for it is a beautiful name. But since many historical works call her by her Christian name "Catherine," that is what will be found most often in this text.

Many people also very correctly refer to Tekakwitha as "Kateri." In Mohawk language, "Catherine" is pronounced more like 'KAT er ee,' but with the "k" and "r" pronounced different. The letter "k" in English is sounded out more like a "g" in Mohawk, while the letter "r" in English is pronounced with a little "l" sound by Mohawk speakers: so, '**GAH** teh lee.'[5] Also, "t" can sound like "d." In writing of her, we could say 'Tekakwitha', or 'Catherine', or 'Kateri.' All are names for the same holy person.

It is difficult to know much about Catherine's father, except that he was probably a kind of chieftain and not a Christian. Yet it is correct to picture him praying for his children, for this was and is the outlook of Native peoples. Life is a gift, and the Iroquois did not forget to give thanks.[6] The Iroquois were harsh in war and toward captives. Their cruelty is well known and it is often mentioned in stories about them. Catherine, early in life, saw the contradiction between thankfulness for life, and cruelty.[7] We will see just a little of how she had the many admirable ways of American Indian people, and how—as with all peoples— the ways become even better when displayed by holy people among them.

---

[5] Allan Greer, *Mohawk Saint; Catherine Tekakwitha and the Jesuits*, Oxford Press, 2005, p. xi.; and also *Blessed Kateri Tekakwitha/North American Indian,* Tekawitha Conference National Center, P.O. Box 6759, Great Falls, MT 59406, no date, 20 pages, cf. p. 10.

[6] Snow, *Op.Cit.*, p.24, speaks of the "Maple Ceremony" as a very early and continuing cultural event. It includes the Thanksgiving Speech that "*marks both the opening and closing of the ceremony.*"

[7] Fr. Chauchetière, *Op.Cit.*, p. 124: "..she could not bear to see anyone harmed, not even a slave, ..."

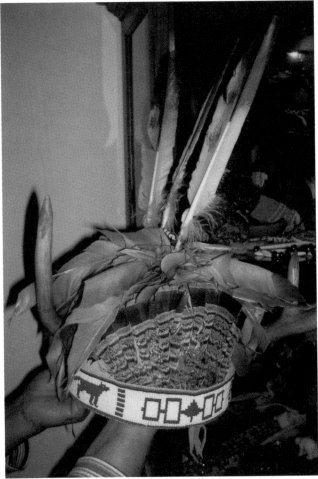

Courtesy of Leona Gonzales

The above is an example of an Iroquois chieftain's headdress, so unlike those with many feathers worn by western chiefs. The bead design is a familiar Mohawk emblem: the several nations united to one another, with the tree as their standard. (The beads here are of the type likely not available in Catherine's time. She would have used sea shells or porcupine quills.)

Women in Mohawk Iroquois society held a prominent authority.[8] Catherine, all would expect, would grow up to be among such important people—the women—in the Mohawk community. And she would be expected to marry and have a family, and pass along her clan identity.

_____

8 Many sources speak of the role of the women elders. Cf. Snow, *Op. Cit.*, pp. 15ff; Margaret Bunson, *Kateri Tekakwitha, Mystic of the Wilderness*, Our Sunday Visitor, Huntington, IN, 1992, p. 33.

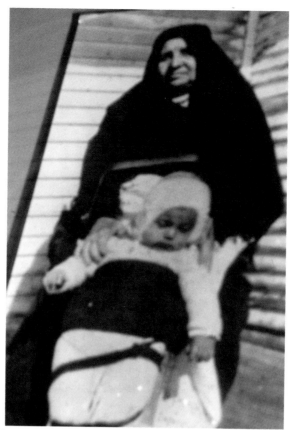

Courtesy of St Francis Xavier Church/Museum, Kahnawake, Canada

Native women and men have always cared deeply for their family's children.

Many things in the lives of women as wives would have appealed to Catherine. They were not the matriarchs that some describe them to be.[9] But they gave stability to their society, had a decided role in the choice of leaders, and were rightly appreciated for their role as food producers.

But even at an early age, Catherine was unique. She saw the world differently.[10] Among other things was her decision about marrying. She was to choose a life that was different, based on her view of what in her own particular life was of the greatest importance.

---

[9] Snow, *Op.Cit.*, p. 65.

[10] Fr. Chauchetière, *Op.Cit.*, p.123.

Photo by E. Sherman at Holy Family Catholic Church, Tuscarora, Reservation, NY.

This cross hangs outside the doorway of the Holy Family Catholic Church, Tuscarora Iroquois Reservation, in western New York. On its crossbeam is the Iroquois emblem. Many feel the blend of Native culture and Christian faith is very proper.

The story of Catherine Tekakwitha is from years ago. Many old-time ways turn out wonderfully good. In her story there is also something new. It is how word was being spread around the earth of the truth the angels brought on the first Christmas night: good news for everyone in the world. That news, of course, started with God, the Creator of all human beings along with everything else. Over thousands of years Native people as well as many others have called God by various names, and through the almost countless centuries people sought the Creator's favor.

Just two thousand years ago—after a period of special preparation which we now know as the Old Testament—God sent His own Son, Jesus Christ, to be Savior of the world. This is the good news, or Gospel, that the angels sang about. Catherine came to know this, for she often heard this Gospel story, and she knew that accepting and believing it was the greatest thing that anyone could ever do.

For a moment let us look ahead. A missionary tells what happened just hours before Catherine's death:

"I am leaving you," said Catherine. "I am about to die. Always remember what we have done together since we knew each other;…. Take courage,…. I will love you in heaven, I will pray for you, I will assist you."[11]

"KO NON RON KWA KA RON IA KE" ("I will love you in heaven.")

"ON KON IE NA WA SE" ("I will help you.")

"ON KON IA TE RON NA ION A SE" ("I will pray for you.")

Even from that time of Catherine's death many in the Catholic Church have held that she was a very holy person. Then, in 1980, Pope John Paul II officially called her "Blessed." Many today yearn for the moment when the Church will officially bestow upon Catherine the title "Saint."

We can find support in this belief because many witnesses remembered her death, which could only be described as beautiful. They could see signs that indicated she went to heaven, for they soon saw people receive blessings from God after asking Catherine to bring God's help upon them. The accumulation of these experiences through the years confirms the belief of a great many people that Catherine has entered into heaven.

But returning to the early part of Catherine's life, we must give attention to her mother, who did not live to an old age. But in those less than half-dozen years she gave Catherine a wonderful beginning. A number of writers say it was the result of her fervent prayers that her daughter was eventually baptized. From age four, the little one might remember her mother. And some evidence seems to show Catherine was a little

---

11 Fr. Chauchetière, *Op. Cit.*, p. 204. The woman Catherine was talking to was her good friend Marie-Thérèse Tegaiaguenta, who remembered much about Catherine's life. Fr. Chauchetière was witness to Katharine's deep spirituality right up to her death, and he himself thereby became almost a changed man. cf. Greer, *Op.Cit.,* pp. 4-5.

older than four when her mother died.[12] But even from the younger age, she could have remembered her mother and felt her influence. A mother is so very important in anyone's life. Native persons—perhaps more than others—see life that way.

Photo by E. Sherman of drawing with permission of Bradley Thompson, Spirit Lake Reservation, ND

Though from a different Native American setting, the above could show how Catherine's memories of her mother stay with her throughout life.

---

[12] 3/20/06 correspondence from Allan Greer.

Being Catholic, Catherine's good mother wanted her children to be baptized, a desire which in itself is a saving thing. And if she had been well enough when the smallpox came, she could have done the Baptism herself, for there may have been no priests in the village at the time.[13] She likely did not know it was permissible for her to do so.

Chapter Two: Smallpox and the Desire for Better Land Meant Moving.

Until about the year 1660 Catherine's family lived in the closest Mohawk village to Ft. Orange. It is remembered as Ossernenon, and it was there where the smallpox enveloped them, leaving the little girl an orphan. Because of that pestilence, and also because the surrounding lands were no longer fertile enough for their food-plantings, that village was abandoned and another village was built just to the west. The name "Gandaouagué I" is how the new place came to be known. But the new village existed only a short time, for it was soon destroyed by a French army attack, and still another village was needed. From about 1667 a "Gandaouagué II," on the north bank of the Mohawk River, became Catherine's home. That site is where Catherine lived till she was 21; it was located near present-day Fonda, New York.

---

13 A Father Simon Le Moyne did sometimes visit the area between 1655 and 1659. (cf. Henry Béchard in *Kateri Takakwitha,* Kateri Center, Kahnawake, Quebec, 1994, p. 22. He quotes R. G. Thwaites, *The Jesuit Relations and Allied Documents*, New York, Pageant Book Company, 1959, Vol. 43, p. 214.)

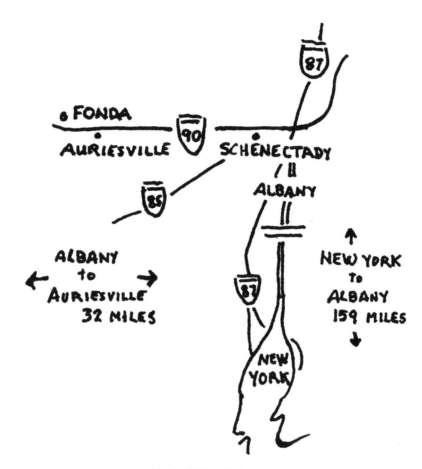

Map by William C. Sherman

The above modern map-sketch of east-central New York shows the places Catherine lived her first 21 years.
Auriesville is near the site of Ossernenon, which now is known as the *National Shrine of North American Martyrs*;
it is found by exiting #27 of Interstate 90 (the New York State Thruway), then taking SR 5S.
Catherine's earliest years of life are commemorated there.
Fonda is the site of Gandaouagué II. After exiting at #28 ("Fonda-Fultonville") from that same Thruway,
enter the town of Fonda, then take Rte 5 going toward the left. The *National Shrine*
of Blessed Kateri Tekakwitha is less than a mile out of town (to the west.)

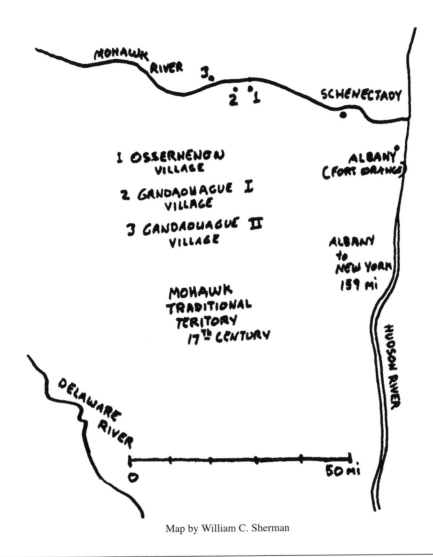

Map by William C. Sherman

Another sketch of the region along the Mohawk River shows the locations of Native villages. They were: Ossernenon, Catherine's birthplace in 1656; Gandaouagué I, where her people moved about 1660, and which was destroyed by the French in 1666; and Gandaouagué II, where Catherine received Baptism at age 19. It was from this last place that, after some time, she made the long journey to her final home near Montreal on the St. Lawrence River.

Courtesy of Fordham University Press, from their *Positio*. Permission received.

A priest enters a longhouse. Missionaries did this with much prayer, many having become proficient in the peoples' language. Those most connected with the times and places of Catherine were the members of the Society of Jesus, the "Jesuits." They were in Canada, among the Hurons. They came also to the Iroquois.

The Iroquois were known as conciliators as they dealt with one another in their confederation. But they were relentless in war with others, and in their treatment of captives. At least one author says that this sometimes harshness of the Iroquois—in seeming contrast to their other efforts—was because of their notion of religion.[14] But here a clarification is necessary. "Religion" is not a clear description of what people go through in similar situations. Modern conflicts are sometimes too quickly said to be from

14 Daniel Sargent, *Catherine Tekakwitha*, Longmans, Green and Co., New York, Toronto, 1940, p. 32.

religious causes. What the Iroquois had been experiencing could demand seeing another side of the picture. In truth they were very hard pressed by diseases, wars, and departures that were taking away many of their people. Grief and mourning may have intensified their harshness. Their wars especially in the years after the coming of the Europeans are sometimes termed "mourning wars."[15]

Mohawks are very often described as a people to be feared. But a look at their view of life deserves our notice. They, and other Iroquoians, hold that the world is composed of good things as well as those which are tainted by evil. They also hold that the proportions of good and evil can change. Good men can become evil as the balance tips, and evil men can be made good by right-minded neighbors.[16] If some accounts of her life make it look as if—except for Catherine—most people were not very good, the Native perspective just mentioned should be remembered. It gives some insight into the character of her caregivers. We know that she grew steadily in goodness, and so at least some of the credit must be given to the family of her birth and of her rearing. Speaking of Catherine and of the way she felt about the uncle who had adopted her, one author says: "(In) his ways, with the keen instinct of little children, she sensed … warmth and affection…"[17]

Just to review the places and times of Catherine's life: she lived her first 21 years in sites along the Mohawk River,[18] then, for her last three years, home was near Montreal, Canada, in a village fairly near the present-day community of Kahnawake. The spelling of that attractive Canadian community presently has two "k's," and local people pronounce them like "g's.": *Gah-na-WA-ge.*

As a little girl Catherine had barely survived smallpox, a malady which left her weak, partially blind, and with her face terribly scarred. But being physically disabled did not hinder her from fully participating in the life of all around her and doing admirable work. She appreciated beautiful things, and made things that brightened the lives of all. This might be surprising, considering her weakened eyes, and the intricacy of

---

15 Greer, *Op. Cit.*, p, 13: *…the only solution to the gnawing sense of loss lay in war and in the integration of enemy captives into the diminished clan.*

16 Dean R. Snow, *op. cit..*, p.5

17 Francis X. Weiser, S.J., *Kateri Takakwitha,* Kateri Center, Kahnawake, Quebec, Canada JOL 1BO, 1972, p.33.

18 These villages were sometimes moved short distances to more fertile agricultural sites.

work in which Catherine excelled. Writers give a vivid picture of Mohawk artistic skill.[19] She was very proficient in all the fine things she did, and that was in spite of having to cover her head with a blanket to shield her weak eyes.[20] That "seclusion"—even though she lived and truly interacted in her rather crowded longhouse[21]—may well have helped her grow in her interior life.

Courtesy of Tekakwitha Conference, Great Falls., MT. Artist: Tisket

Catherine gives us one of her lasting examples of striving for goodness: her quest of the spiritual, rather than giving undue attention to matters that have no lasting value. Beautiful things she could think about

---

[19] A further description of Mohawk artistic work is found in pp. 34-43 of Greer, *Op. Cit.*

[20] Fr. Chauchetière, *Op. Cit.*, p.120. The name Tekakwitha may come from her often "feeling her way."

[21] Although Katharine later wished to have a plain appearance, she did wear beads, as the other girls did, even for a while after her baptism. Cf. *Ibid.*, p. 170

and dwell on. At our modern time she would almost surely urge turning off excessive stimuli such as too much media or video games.

Catherine was not disturbed by her handicap; she was always kind,[22] even patiently accepted whatever came her way.[23] She seemed to know that somehow good would come and that God would provide.

Courtesy of Fordham University Press, from their *Positio*. Permission received.

A Mohawk girl of that time is shown performing duties in fields and at home.

An uncle and two aunts, by Native custom, had taken on Catherine's care. The dozen or more years that followed are ones that need more study. But such a consideration is difficult, for the records of that time

---

[22] *Ibid.*, p.124: "..she could not bear to see anyone harmed,..."

[23] When a false story was told about her: "*...she remained patient, meek and humble, and left her reputation ... in the hands of God, ...*" *Ibid.* p.192. Catherine was never anything but forgiving.

period are scarce. Some stories of her life describe those years as a time when she was treated harshly. When that happened, it likely was because of her wanting to stay unmarried. Father Chauchetière writes:

> *Her relatives, however, wished to see her established, and urged her to marry, whereas she did not wish to do so. In order to rid themselves of her, and because she was looked upon as an ill-favored slave who would become a burden on the cabin, they sent her from lodge to lodge.*[24]

Chapter Three: Catherine's Life Before and Up To Age Nineteen

We may never know fully just how much affection Catherine received during her childhood. How valuable it would be if she had written of her own experiences! She didn't, and in fact she couldn't do such a thing, for her people had no custom of writing as we think of it today.

From what we have said before, it seems almost certain that while she was a young girl, Catherine's family and other relatives treated her with love and care. It was when she grew a little older that they started to get displeased because of her decision to remain unmarried. And there was opposition to her becoming Christian as well. Father Cholenec tells of her, at about age 19, when she first openly talked to a priest about getting baptized:

> *She disclosed… the obstacles she had been obliged to surmount on the part of her family,….*[25]

Yet Catherine must have received loving care as a child. A look at what happened in the life of another well-known person, Thérèse of Lisieux, who received much love, can serve as grounds for the belief that Catherine received similar loving care.

---

[24] Fr. Chauchetière, *Op.Cit.*, p. 123.

[25] Fr. Peter Cholenec, *Positio* Document XII, 1715, p. 349

Saint Thérèse of Lisieux (France), 1873-1897
Courtesy of Pope John Paul II Cultural Center, Washington, DC

Catherine (Kateri) Tekakwitha, 1656-1680
Courtesy of St. Francis Xavier, Kahnawake, Canada

In the lives of Catherine Tekakwitha and St. Thérèse of Lisieux, whom many know as 'the Little Flower,'
many things were similar, from their earliest years onward.

The lives of Catherine and Saint Thérèse are so much alike that they almost demand making comparisons. The writer of this text will propose that noting these likenesses is not only enlightening, but also justifiable. Though many years separate the lives of Catherine and Thérèse, they are alike time after time. Both remained unmarried; both had a wonderful way of praying; both died at age 24.

But a remarkable early similarity is that when both of the two were very young girls, their mothers died, and the girls were deprived of their mothers' care. Catherine did not ever write about this. But Thérèse did write, and she tells how difficult were the ten years after her mother's death, and only with the help of her loving family was she able to struggle through those years.[26] After Catherine lost her mother, she couldn't write to tell anyone about this, but her subsequent rearing also must have been with love. She hardly would have become a wonderful young woman and adult without some very important people in her family treating her well.[27] Admittedly Catherine's adopting family has sometimes been characterized as being harsh.[28] But she could very well have sensed that the step-father, especially, cared about her. She likely received strength of character from him, for time after time she herself was strong-minded in living the commandments and doing what she was convinced was God's will for her.

Catherine's strong-mindedness appears even in her early teens, for she displayed great determination to remain unmarried. Though Iroquois teenage girls had some freedom about accepting a proposed marriage,[29] it took courage for her to continue to resist all pressure to choose the married way of life. Father Chauchetière writes of a time she was pressured:

> *When she was old enough to be married, they wished to surprise her. They sent into her lodge a young man who had been told to sit beside her. When he came, they told Catherine to offer him some sagamite, pretending that he spoke of marrying her, and thus force her to go with him as her husband. Catherine left the lodge and hid in the fields. The affair was pushed further and they tried again to compromise her, but she cleverly hid behind a cache of Indian corn.*[30]

---

[26] cf. *The Story of a Soul,* St. Thérèse of Lisieux's autobiography, TAN Books and Publications, —Rockford IL, 1997, pp. 18ff.

[27] A qualified comparison with Thérèse may be appropriate. Natives saw other relatives as very close. Their word even for "mother" applied to mother's sisters as well. Cf. Snow, *Op Cit.*, p. 15.

[28] Father Edward LeCompte, S. J., *Glory of the of the Mohawks,* Bruce, Milwaukee, 1944, p. 44 has: "It was a source of great chagrin to him that he could not control her."

[29] Greer, *Op.Cit.*, page 46.

[30] Fr. Chauchetière, *Op.Cit.*, page 125. Sagamite (Sagamité): the French version of an Algonquin word for a prepared corn dish. At that special time, a woman's presenting of a bowl of sagamite could be seen as willingness to marry.

Courtesy of Leona Gonzales

Native Americans were the first to cultivate corn, a real staple food for most, if not all, Native people.
Tuscarora corn was of this light-colored variety.

It was quite expected that young women marry. Some might have seen Catherine's decision to remain unmarried as outright defiance. For even though, as already mentioned, Mohawk women were not at all powerless, this particular decision of Catherine was even more far-reaching. And it indicates that she felt she had some real "say" about her own life. To maintain that position, from time to time she even had to go counter to the admonitions of other and older women.[31] Her choosing the life that she did could even foreshadow the insight of a revered later-day Iroquois teacher who said that some things outweigh even the bond between mother and daughter.[32] And her outlook is also consistent with Christ's teaching about

---

[31] Fr. Cholenec, *Positio* Document X, 1696, p. 278. Even elderly and motherly Anastasia Tagonhatsiongo, at a later time and in this regard, did not prevail over Catherine.

[32] Snow, *Op.cit.*, p. 162. The personal name of the teacher was "Handsome Lake"; he was first prominent in the early 19th century. How he arrived at his whole body of teachings and where they have led, is to this day a deep study for well-informed Christian and non-Christian Iroquois alike.

"leaving father and mother,"[33] and choosing a rightful life even when parents or elders wrongly interfere.

Photo by E. Sherman at Kateri Shrine and Indian Museum, Fonda, NY.

A display on the grounds of the shrine near Fonda, New York, displays the words of an Iroquois teacher still well known.

Catherine would not allow herself to languish with feelings of self-pity, or to claim that her disabilities excused her from participating in the life of the longhouse. Father Chauchetière writes:

Catherine's duties were to gather firewood with her aunt, to tend the fire when her mother ordered her, to get water when those in the lodge needed it. …. People who knew her from her childhood said that she was intelligent and skilful, especially with her hands, …. If I can judge by the objects which I saw her make, I should say that she worked daintily in pigskin and deerskin.[34] She made belts in which the … women and girls carry wood, and those which the ancients used in negotiating the affairs of the nation, made of …beads[35]. …. She was also skilful in making ribbons …from the skins of eels or from

33 Matthew 19:5.

34 "pigskin and deerskin": the Jesuits are talking of porcupine quills and moosehide. (3/20/06 correspondence from Allan Greer.)

35 The belts "used in the affairs of the nation" are called *wampum*. They were (also) made of shells.

thick tree-bark. These she colored red with the glue from sturgeons which are plentiful among the Iroquois. …. She made baskets and boxes and the buckets used for drawing water. Her skill, therefore, was such that she always had some occupation to fall back on.

Courtesy of Leona Gonzales

Porcupine quills were used very daintily to make beautiful objects. Catherine made such things.

Sometimes she made an instrument for grinding Indian corn, sometimes she made matting from tree-bark, and sometimes she made poles for stacking corn. In addition to these occupations, there were her daily tasks in the service of the others – grinding corn for soup and bread and serving the food in abundance. Although she was infirm, she was always the first to be at work. She spent some years before her baptism performing these daily tasks ….[36]

---

36 Fr. Chauchetière, *Op.Cit.*, pp. 122-124.

Courtesy of St. Francis Xavier Church/Museum, Kahnawake Reserve, Canada

Corn was ground into fine particles using a stout piece of wood almost like a bat, and a stump with a hollowed top.

…what progress Catherine made …. The Holy Ghost … led her, … so that she pleased both God and the world; for even the worst respected her and the best found in her a worthy model.[37]

---

37 *Ibid*, p. 142.

Chapter Four: Catherine's Catholic Life Begins.

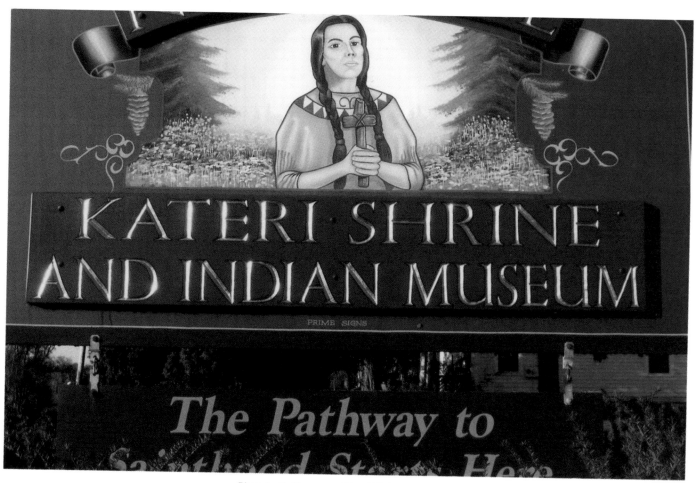

Photo by E. Sherman at Kateri Shrine, Fonda, NY.

Rte 5 Highway just west of Fonda has this welcoming sign, informing the travelers that they have arrived at the National Shrine of Blessed Kateri Tekakwitha, Fonda, NY 12068, telephone 518-853-3646.

Because Catherine always wanted to do God's will, the Holy Spirit was with her in the years before she was baptized. In God's providence, the Holy Spirit may come to a person even before Baptism. The Catholic Church teaches: "…the desire for Baptism (can) bring(s) about the fruits of Baptism…."[38]

A comparison of Catherine with St. Thérèse of Lisieux has already been made, and the following is another similarity. It is well known that Thérèse saw the practise of charity (love) to be the most important virtue for the followers of Jesus. She was named a "Doctor of the Church" by Pope John Paul II, because she taught this so clearly by her words and by her example. Yet two hundred years before Thérèse was even born, Father Cholenec wrote the following about Catherine:

…I have already given some beautiful examples of her virtues, …. I wish to say a little more concerning that one which is most admirable in the Saints, and which is the only virtue conducive to real sanctity. Charity is not only the queen of virtues, enriching all others, but it is also the source of sanctity, the shortest and safest road to holiness and perfection, since it is only necessary, according to Saint Paul, to love God with one's whole heart to attain that end.[39]

(Her) one thought was to find out what was most agreeable to God.[40]

---

[38] The Catechism of the Catholic Church, #1258.

[39] Fr. Cholenec, *Positio* Document X, 1696, p. 290. Cf. 1 Corinthians, 13:1-13. Father Cholenec, as Catherine's chief instructor, would have given her insights into this Holy Scripture.

[40] Fr. Chauchetière, *Op. Cit.*, page 171.

Photo by E. Sherman at St. Peter's Church of the Kateri Shrine, Fonda, NY

A scene from St. Peter's Chapel near Fonda presents a vivid depiction of the providential opportunity Catherine had to tell of her desire to be baptized Christian. It shows the priest coming by, not knowing she was in the lodge.

God, in an unexpected way brought a priest into Catherine's life, Father de Lamberville. The occasion is described by Father Cholenec:

At length when she least expected it(,)the occasion of her declaring her desire for Baptism presented itself. A wound which she had received in the foot detained her in the village whilst the greater part of

the women were in the fields gathering the harvest of Indian corn. The missionary[41] had selected this time to go his rounds and instruct at his leisure those who had remained in the cabins. He entered that of Tegahkouita. This good girl on seeing him was not able to restrain her joy. She at once began to open her heart to him, even in the presence of her companions, on the earnest desire she had to be admitted into the fold of the Christians. She disclosed also the obstacles she had been obliged to surmount on the part of her family, and in this first conversation showed …courage….[42]

Courtesy of Simon Brascoupe, artist

The above is by Tuscarora/Algonquin/Mohawk artist, Simon Brascoupe. It is at the Native American Museum of Art (NAMA) on the Tuscarora Reservation: 2293 Saunders Settlement Rd, Sanborn NY 14132. Permission has been sought.

---

41 This was Father James de Lamberville. cf. *Positio* Document III, 1682, p. 79.

42 Fr. Cholenec, *Positio* Document XII, 1715, pp. 348-349

God protects and governs all things.[43] This care, which sometimes takes faith to see, is spoken of as "divine providence." Catherine saw good things happen, and so many of them came about because of the people God brought into her life. And in turn, she believed that the things that happened to her would bring good to the world around her. Events inspired by God opened the way for Catherine to prepare for Baptism.

Courtesy of Tekakwitha Conference, P.O. Box 6768, Great Falls, MT 59409

This drawing shows Catherine using her skills in the beautiful Mohawk ways.
(This is also one of the very rare portrayals that show how fully her face was covered with scars.)

---

43 *Catechism of the Catholic Church*, #302

Father Cholenec writes:

...(Since)...Catherine, ... , could not suffer the broad daylight on account of the weakness of her eyes, her aunts ...entrusted her with the care of the lodge ....the missionary..., making his regular visits at the lodges..., felt inspired to ... enter there. He ...found the young girl, who showed extraordinary pleasure in this visit for which she had longed so much. The Father on his side was most edified by her modesty and reserve, but he was even more so when he had spoken with her and had learned what a virtuous life she led. He was delighted to discover so many virtues in...(her.)

He recognized clearly that the Holy Ghost had enlightened the eyes of her soul to see, and had touched her heart to embrace the truth of our religion. For this reason he resolved and promised, at this first interview, to grant her the grace she so ardently desired, I mean Baptism. After having passed the entire winter in teaching her thoroughly and preparing her to receive this sacrament, they appointed a day for it;....[44]

From the above we can see that the missionary Father de Lamberville did not wish to defer Catherine's Baptism for long. He saw also that the Native Christians were happy when he decided to baptize her at the Mohawk village. Father Chauchetière writes:

After Catherine had persevered some time in going to pray as a catechumen, the priest thought of baptizing her. He wished to proceed with the matter.... ...he yet moderated his desire to baptize her. On the other hand, he did not wish to defer this Baptism ..., for he feared to deprive God of a soul so dear to Him. For some days he made a careful inquiry into the life and customs of the girl. Those of Catherine's lodge spoke only good of her and the people of the village did likewise, and all the Christians rejoiced when the priest finally decided to baptize her. When the news concerning her Baptism was brought to her she was exceedingly happy. She had learned her prayers with a quickness and eagerness which was truly marvelous, out of fear that Baptism might be refused her under the pretext that she had not had enough instruction.

---

44 Fr. Cholenec, *Positio* Document X, 1696 p. 244-245.

Father Chauchetière's words continue:

> *The priest chose Easter Sunday [1676] as the time and the chapel as the place for such a solemn Baptism. Together with two others Catherine was baptized with all the ceremonies of the Church. She was given the name of Catherine. ......The Holy Ghost, entering into Catherine at Baptism, ..., placed her among the souls of the elect and raised her in four years to a high degree of holiness.*[45]

The Divine Son of God became human when He was conceived and born of the Virgin Mary. At about the age of 33, on what we now call Good Friday, He was put on a cross, and there He died. But as He had foretold, He rose on the third day, Easter. With both soul and body, He is fully alive.

Easter is a very fitting, though not the only time, for Baptism. That sacrament gives holiness to each person in both soul and body, united with Jesus. Then God can continue His help, and each person can live a holy life, which means being forever with Our Lord. Heaven is the goal for which every baptized person must strive, for the good of their souls. Actually it is even more than that, for each person's body will be eventually raised up too, and it will be united with their soul, whole and beautiful, in heaven for ever more.

For the sake of her soul, Catherine was really hard on her own body here in this world, accepting and even making it suffer. She kept thinking how much Jesus had suffered, and how He still has the marks of those sufferings. But now the marks of those suffering are healed, and in glory. That is the way it is for Catherine now. Her years of love, often with frightful suffering, are now forever fulfilled in heaven. Easter is very real for her, and so it must be for everyone who is baptized.

The Fonda, New York, shrine is now accepted as being very close to the village where Catherine and her family lived and where she was baptized. Located on a well-conditioned highway, the shrine is very accessible, and all interested visitors are welcome there. Persons wishing to feel a sense of Catherine's presence and her emerging holiness might do well to stop at this shrine and nearby locations. People can

---

[45] Fr. Chauchetière, *Op. Cit.*, pp. 136, 137.

Photo by E. Sherman at St. Peter's Church of Kateri Shrine, Fonda, NY

An old drawing in the Fonda shrine's St. Peter's Church illustrates Father de Lamberville baptizing Catherine, calling her by that name. Her Catholic Christian friends joyfully welcomed her and served as her godparents. She was nineteen years of age.

even climb just a half-mile to a higher level, and come to the most thoroughly studied of all past Iroquois villages. It went by the name "Caughnawaga," but is more recently referred to as "Gandaouagué." This is the locale where Catherine lived for many years and where she was baptized.

Photo by E. Sherman, at Kateri Shrine, Fonda, NY

A sign near the Fonda shrine gift shop points to the place of Catherine's adolescent years, and then her Baptism.

Early in this book is a sketch showing longhouses and the way some were grouped within the village walls. That drawing was made according to what archeologists found just a half mile from the Fonda shrine. Remains in the ground clearly showed investigators the size and location of the houses and the village's double wall. Stakes of different colors are now in place, marking the walls and various furnishings of that community. There one can imagine the events in Catherine's life in these well-outlined places.

Photo by E. Sherman near Kateri Shrine, Fonda, NY

Just above the hill from the Fonda shrine the Gandaouagué village has been found. In the 1940's, the attempts to find evidence seemed to be failing, but Father Thomas Grassmann and the New York State Archeological Association continued work, and by 1956 the whole village and its surrounding walls were clearly revealed. This sign provides technical details.

Catherine showed nothing but love for her relatives and all others in the village where she lived, but there were difficulties ahead. At first her aunts—her adopting mothers—seemed to accept her decision to become

Catholic.[46] They may have thought she would then agree to being married. But as time went by, even the practice of her adopted Christianity became difficult; some children as well as others began to ridicule her. An attempt by a young man to scare her is often mentioned in stories of her life.[47] There is some reason to believe that he did not intend to harm her.[48] But even though she likely felt her steadfastness would mean death, she would not give up her faith, and was willing to accept martyrdom.

Courtesy of Fordham University Press, from their *Positio*. Permission received.

This is a dramatized portrayal of how opponents tried to frighten Catherine into giving up her Catholic ways.
Yet this threat did not make her yield.

46 Fr. Cholenec, *Positio* Document XII, 1715, p. 350.

47 Fr. Chauchetière, *Op.Cit.,* p. 140.

48 Greer, *Op.Cit.,* p. 56.

The missionary, Father de Lamberville, urged Catherine to move from Gandaouagué, but she wanted to be loyal to her relatives and to her tribe.[49] Likely all this time others had been going away, but Catherine continued in the traditional Mohawk region for over a year. It was only through an arrangement made by several Christian Iroquois that she finally agreed to make the long journey to Canada. Some written accounts describe this as a fleeing. Clearly the uncle who had become her father did not want her to move away. But she had not committed herself to a husband, and she was entitled to make decisions for herself. She wanted to be in a place where she could take part more completely in daily Catholic life. Looking at the details of her decision to go to Canada, the writer of this text feels it is not correct to describe that departure by saying that she fled as some kind of coward. She was not one to turn from holiness even if there was reason to fear for her life.

---

[49] Fr. Francis de Charlevoix, S.J., *History and General Description of New France, (Positio* Document XVII, 1744, pp. 424-425.) "*She was …sensitive to the reproach made that she had no affection for her kindred, that she hated her tribe, and gave… her attachment to the one to which her mother belonged.*"

Courtesy of Fordham University Press, from their *Positio*. Permission received.

Catherine made the tiring journey of several hundred miles north from her Mohawk River village to the St. Lawrence River.

A prominent Oneida, having made a trip to Mohawk country for the explicit purpose of speaking enthusiastically about his new-found Christianity, arranged for Catherine's departure. Accounts of this have been made very dramatic, with Catherine's step-father portrayed as ready to murder the "abductors." His alleged anger is quite understandable, even if not fully justified. He did not want Catherine to move away, but preferred that she marry, bringing another warrior-hunter to be among the family's relatives. He saw they were losing her. He did not understand why she felt so deeply about this Jesus Christ, whom she had come to know. But he did know that this adopted daughter was as fine and as holy as anyone could ever want to be part of one's life. But now this good young woman, likely so similar to the woman from the north who had become the wife of his brother, was moving away to the north herself. If only we had written words from Catherine! She surely must have hated to have him hurt![50] She must have deeply wanted blessings for him, and all her relatives, in her decision.

Chapter Five: Catherine Begins Life in Canada

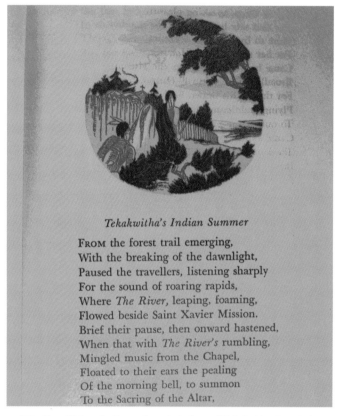

Courtesy of Fordham University Press, from their *Song of Tekakwitha*. Permission received.

Catherine arrived and was welcomed at her new home near the St. Lawrence River.

---

[50] Comparisons with St. Thérèse were made earlier, and another parallel may also be justified. Thérèse realized that her own personal calling meant leaving her father. But she never forgot him, remembering him with love, and suffering real anguish when she did not know his situation. (Cf. *Story of a Soul*, Op. cit., pp. 132-133.) Our Catherine must have also.

The remaining three years of Catherine's life were in Canada, at the St. Xavier Christian Iroquois Mission on the south bank of the St. Lawrence River near Montreal. The river at that point roared in turbulent rapids. The French word for rapids is "sault" (pronounced 'SOO'), and the Native village in Canada to which Catherine went is often spoken of as in French: "The Sault," in Mohawk: "Kahnawake." People there could fully live their faith and daily take part in the practices of Catholic life. They welcomed newly arrived people and helped them establish themselves and make the community their home. For them, and the newly-arrived Catherine, this meant doing the daily work that life required.

photo by E. Sherman

In modern St. Catherine, Quebec, along the St Lawrence River, the street name makes reference to the rapids in that great river, which is barely showing through the trees.

Food had to be grown, gathered and preserved. Clothing had to be made primarily with their own skilled hands, though European items did at times come their way. The Iroquois had to provide for themselves, as all Natives had done through the centuries. In those Canadian years, Catherine took a very active part in all these activities. At the same time, her new surroundings and her new neighbors made her able to embrace the Christian life ever more perfectly. The people in the village helped Catherine, and some especially deserve to be given mention. One person, moreover, has to have a place in this account, though he would likely have refused praise for the wonderful things that happened, and might say that he was simply a witness. He does declare that the events which he witnessed—and also helped come about—deeply affected him. This person was the Jesuit missionary priest, Father Claude Chauchetière.

View of the Residence of the Jesuit Fathers in the College of Poitiers, Drawn from the Garden, 1699. Bibliothèque nationale de France, Va86, tome 3. © Photograph Bibliothèque nationale de France, Paris.

Courtesy of Allan Greer, from his *Mohawk Saint*

Father Chauchetière began receiving his schooling in his hometown of Poitiers, France. It was there also that he had some of his more advanced preparations to become a member of the Society of Jesus (the Jesuits). This was their residence in Poitiers.

Father Claude, like the other missionaries, was from the "Old World," and had come to America from Europe. The "worlds" of Europe and of America were very different. America was called the "New World." This was said sometimes with condescension or disdain, but sometimes with curiosity and admiration. In seeking more fully to understand the French perspective, a look at an often-used French word can help. In talking about, or describing Native people, the French used the word "sauvage." English translators frequently transformed that into "savage." This text will not use that English word, for it has come to connote brutality or uncivilized. A review will show that the French writers of the 17th and later centuries by no means always intended "sauvage" to have a derogatory connotation.

Photo by E. Sherman

So much of the western hemisphere was wooded. It is no accident that the French described it as "sauvage."
That word is derived from the Latin "silva," meaning "forest."

By using the word "sauvage" many writers tried to convey the idea of being untouched, pristine, or unspoiled. Rather than the unfortunate and inaccurate English word "savage," used by an older linguist when translating a phrase from the French, we can find a more recent scholar translating "sauvage" differently, saying simply "Indian."[51]

The way that some of the noblest of Europeans, the missionaries, viewed the people or the land was bound to color what they observed, preserved and wrote. It is, therefore, valuable to know their outlook, and especially that of Father Chauchetière, who deserves our attention because of his witness and his writings.

There is evidence that Father Claude Chauchetière was having a hard time in his new environment. In addition, he does not seem to have had great confidence in himself. He may have wondered if his endeavors in America would result in much good.[52] But his pastoral duties brought him to "The Sault" in 1677, the same year Catherine arrived, and there he observed a marvel he cherished for the rest of his life. He was present at the very instant of Catherine's death. Before her death, and especially at its very moment, the priest sensed the union she had with God. This inspired him for the rest of his life, and he was quite driven to tell and write of her life, and of her grace-filled death. He was favored, we are told, with a later vision of Catherine in which she told him to let people know about the wonders of her faith.[53]

---

[51] Greer, *Op. Cit.*, p. 52: "(Catherine) was given the baptismal name of Catherine, a popular name 'held in great veneration among the Indians.'" vs. the *Positio* translation of Fr. Chauchetière, p. 154: "The name of Catherine was 'held in great veneration among the savages;'"

[52] Greer, *Op. Cit.*, pp. 81-82; Henry Béchard, *Kateri Tekahkwitha,* Kateri Center, Kahnawake, Quebec, 1994, p. 91.

[53] Fr. Cholenec, *Positio* Document X, 1696, pp. 311-312.

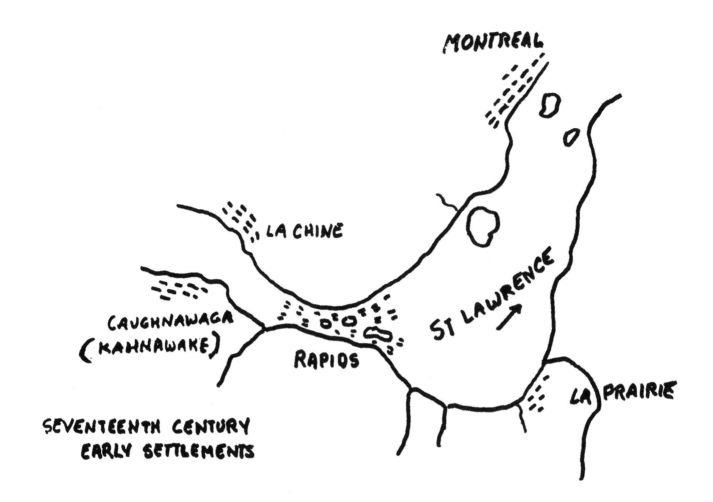

MONTREAL

LA CHINE

CAUGHNAWAGA
(KAHNAWAKE)

RAPIOS

ST LAWRENCE

LA PRAIRIE

SEVENTEENTH CENTURY
EARLY SETTLEMENTS

map by William C. Sherman

Since the scene has shifted to Canada, the above is a sketch of a section of the St. Lawrence River. On the south bank of that great river, near a roaring rapids, was the Saint Xavier Christian Iroquois Mission, often referred to as "The Sault." Catherine arrived in that locality at age 21 from Gandaouagué in New York. Later—actually in the early eighteenth century—today's Kahnawake was built farther west, and it is there that her tomb can be found today.

Having been baptized before coming to Canada, Catherine normally would be given the sacrament of Confirmation, yet there is no record of her receiving it. In 1676, the Bishop of Quebec did confirm hundreds of Native people at the "The Sault," but Catherine was not listed in those records.[54] If she never received Confirmation—and the bishop lived far away[55]—it is certainly regrettable.

The very desire for a sacrament can bring graces,[56] but the actual reception is much better. Catherine would be the first to urge people to be confirmed and to welcome the life-long graces God thus gives.

Courtesy of Allan Greer, from his *Mohawk Saint*

> This is an early sketch of the Bishop of Quebec giving Confirmation in 1676. (cf. Greer, *Op. Cit*., p. 103.)
> But for Catherine, who arrived later, there is no record of her Confirmation.

---

[54] Fr. Chauchetière, (not from Document VIII, but from *Positio* Document IV, pp. 96, 97.)

[55] At that time in the Church's history it may have been felt that only a bishop should confirm.

[56] Cf. *Catechism of the Catholic Church*, #1258. Though that paragraph refers to Baptism, hopefully it fits Confirmation too.

Confirmation is for the completion of baptismal grace, with a greater outpouring of the Holy Spirit.[57] Father Chauchetière says that the Holy Ghost (that is, the Holy Spirit) entered Catherine at her Baptism.[58] That is true at each person's Baptism. Yet in retrospect it seems right to assume that concern for Catherine's well-being included wanting her to be confirmed so she could receive an even greater share in the graces of the Holy Spirit. Yet records do not give any proof of such an event.

Courtesy of Allan Greer, from his *Mohawk Saint*

This is an early sketch of the building of the village chapel about 1677 or 1678. The three small figures sitting in the background are possibly Catherine, Marie Skarichions, and best friend Marie-Thérèse Tegaiaguenta, encouraging each other in holiness, and perhaps even talking of forming themselves into a group to be like nuns. (cf. Greer, *Op.Cit.*, p.. 136.)

---

57 *Catechism of the Catholic Church*, #1285.

58 Fr. Chauchetière, *Op. Cit.*, page 137.

But Catherine had learned that God dwelled within her, and wished her to share His constant love. That she realized this, Father Cholenec writes in a passage containing her own words:

One day, while (a friend)[Marie-Thérèse Tegaiaguenta] *was looking at the new church then building at the Sault (the mission which before had been at Prairie de la Madeleine, had been moved here), (the friend) met with Catherine, who was also inspecting it. They saluted each other for the first time, … entering into conversation,…. "Alas," answered Catherine, with a sigh, "it is not in this material temple that God most loves to dwell. It is within ourselves that He wishes to take up his abode. Our hearts are the temple which is most agreeable to Him…."*[59]

Photo by Rudy Gonzales

Above is Mrs. Leona Gonzales. She is Tuscarora, and a devout mother and teacher. Soon in the actual life of Catherine, an Anastasia begins to instruct her in the faith. Mrs. Gonzales resembles Anastasia in many ways.
(The reader can see that the scene above is not the rapids on the St. Lawrence, but Niagara Falls, where Mrs. Gonzales and her husband Rudy were so gracious to take their guest, the writer of this text.)

---

[59] Fr. Cholenec, *Positio* Document XII, 1715, p. 362.

Soon after Catherine arrived at the Sault, Father Peter Cholenec began to see that she got the continued instructions needed to follow her Baptism. These instructions were to prepare her for the sacraments of Penance and Holy Eucharist.[60] Father Cholenec asked the assistance of a very holy local woman, Anastasia Tegonhatsiongo, who had years before known Catherine and had even seen her mother.[61] Father Cholenec himself later wrote:

After arriving at the Sault, Catherine went to live at the home of her brother-in-law, who had brought her into the country. The mistress of the cabin was an old Christian, Anastasia by name, who was among the first of the Iroquois to be baptized by our Fathers. She was one of the pillars of the mission, ...and of the entire village, the one who knew best how to instruct.[62]

Photo by E. Sherman of a confessional at another early Indian mission (Cataldo in northern Idaho)

[60] Fr. Cholenec, *Positio* Document X, 1696, p. 249.

[61] Fr. Chauchetière, *Op. Cit.*, p. 169.

[62] Fr. Cholenec, *Positio* Document X, pp. 249-250. (The "brother-in-law" was the husband of Catherine's <u>adopted</u> sister. That sister will appear later, strongly urging Catherine to marry.)

Photo by E. Sherman

This scene is of the Mohawk River near where Catherine earlier lived.
It can illustrate the peacefulness that the sacrament of Penance is meant to bring.

Sometime, in her new surroundings, Catherine began to go to confession, the sacrament presently also known as Penance or Reconciliation. Father Chauchetière writes:

(Catherine) went to confession weekly, received Holy Communion as often as possible, and made Spiritual Communions frequently during the day.[63]

---

[63] Fr, Chauchetière, *Op.Cit.*, p. 175.

And Father Cholenec also tells of Catherine's practise:

Her fervor was no less evident in the confessions which she made every eight days or sometimes oftener. ..... She thought herself the greatest sinner in the world. It was with such sentiments of humility that she made all her confessions.[64]

Courtesy of the Apostleship of Prayer

Jesus said: "Peace I leave with you; my peace I give to you. Not as the world gives do I give it to you." John 14:27.

[64] Fr. Cholenec, *Positio* Document III, 1996, p. 81.

Chapter Six: Catherine and the Holy Eucharist

Catherine's baptism, and then her confessions, led to what the Catholic Church sees as the noblest of all the sacraments, Holy Eucharist with Holy Communion. Numerous writings describe Catherine's eagerness and fervor in receiving Holy Communion. Father Cholenec writes:

She [Catherine] *received the good news with all imaginable joy, and prepared herself for the great event with an increase of devotion suitable to the exalted idea she had of it. … at this First Communion all her fervor was renewed. The ground was so well prepared that only the approach of this divine fire was necessary, to receive all its warmth.*

Photo by E. Sherman at Holy Family Church, Tuscarora Reservation, New York

This statue of Mary has a place near a tabernacle of her Son,
along with an eagle feather which helps in "smudging," to purify and prepare.

(Catherine) approached or rather surrendered herself to this furnace of sacred love that burns on our altars, and she came out of it so glowing with its divine fire that only Our Lord knew what passed between Himself and His dear spouse during her First Communion. …from that day forward she appeared different to us, because she remained so full of God and of love of Him.

And Father Cholenec continues with further glowing words:

All this will seem very surprising …, but it will seem even more so … that, having afterwards had the happiness of receiving Holy Communion frequently, she always did so with the same disposition and fervor she had the first time, and undoubtedly she received the same love and manifold graces from Our Lord, who seeks only to visit us in this Sacrament of Love, and who puts no limits to His grace, when He comes in contact with hearts disposed to receive and profit by them, as was the case with Catherine.

This fact, moreover, was so well known in the village that at the time of general Communion the most devout women hastened to place themselves near her in church, claiming that the mere sight of her exterior was so devotional and ardent at those times that her example inspired them and served as an excellent preparation for approaching the Holy Table in a proper manner.[65]

Catherine knew Jesus' love, and that He forgave any and all of her sins.

---

[65] Fr. Cholenec, *Positio* Document X, 1696, pp. 255-256.

Courtesy of St. Francis Church/museum, Kahnawake Reserve, Canada

The above statue is at the St. Francis Xavier Church museum in Kahnawake across from Montreal.
Though it does not portray Catherine terribly scarred—as she certainly was—it gives some glimpse of her devotion.

In another passage, Father Cholenec says:

The same fervor was especially evident every time she received Holy Communion. Those who come from the Iroquois are tried out for a long time before they are granted this grace; but it was not so with our Catherine. She had so well prepared herself and she desired this favor so ardently, that it was granted to her forthwith. She made ready for the great day by extraordinary redoubling of her devotion and afterward she seemed altogether different, so much was she filled with God and His holy love. One had not to be long in her company to feel it and to be surrounded by it as she was. All her joy was to think upon Our Lord and to converse familiarly with Him. She passed almost the entire day, on Sundays and feast days, praying at the foot of the altar, and on working days she often came there to offer up her work. If sometimes asked, "Catherine, do you love Our Lord?" – it was enough to see her immediately quite overcome. "Ah, my Father! Ah, my Father!" she would say, and she could say no more.[66]

Catherine had said: *"…it is not in this material temple that God most loves to dwell…"* Nevertheless she knew the chapel was a very holy place, and she visited her Lord there every chance she could. She would come early in the morning, when the unheated holy place was freezing cold.

Courtesy of St. Francis Church/museum, Kahnawake Reserve, Canada

---

[66] Fr. Cholenec's words in *Positio* Document III, 1682, pp. 81-82.

Courtesy of Fordham University Press, from their *Positio*. Permission received.

In the village chapel Catherine continually came to commune with Jesus in the Blessed Sacrament.

Father Cholenec tells us:

From thence [that is, instructions by Anastasia] *arose the … devotion she had for the Holy Eucharist and for the Passion of Our Savior. These two mysteries of the love of the same God, concealed under the veil of the Eucharist and His dying on the cross, ceaselessly occupied her spirit, and kindled in her heart the purest flames of love. Every day she was seen to pass whole hours at the foot of the altar, immovable, as if transported beyond herself. Her eyes often explained the sentiments of her breast by the abundance of tears she shed, and in these tears she found so great delight that she was, as it were, insensible to the most severe cold of winter. Often seeing her benumbed with cold, I have sent her to the cabin to warm herself. She obeyed immediately, but the moment after, returned to the church, and continued there in long communion with Jesus Christ.*[67]

Courtesy of Fordham University Press, from their *Positio*. Permission received.

Wherever she went, Catherine kept in mind the sufferings of Jesus,
often carrying a cross on her person or mounting one on a tree.

During one winter at the Sault, Catherine dutifully lived and worked many days and nights with those going far into the forest in search of game. Out there she was not able to get to Mass, which was the high point of her life. At village Mass times she begged her guardian angel to go, and to bring back blessings.

---

67 Fr. Cholenec, *Positio* Document XII, 1715, p. 372,,

Photo by E. Sherman. Used by permission.

North Dakota Spirit Lake Dakota Sioux children fittingly stand before the figure of St. Michael the Archangel, who battles all evil. Catholic faith also teaches that each of God's children has a guardian angel who continually stays at their side.

Father Cholenec writes:

After the morning prayers, … Catherine retired to solitude to pray again, approximately at the time that the Indians heard Mass at the mission. For this purpose she had erected a small shrine on the bank of a stream. It consisted of a cross she made from a tree. There she joined in spirit the people of the village, uniting her intentions to those of the priests and prayed to her Guardian Angel to be present there in her place and to bring her the fruits of the Holy Sacrifice.[68]

Those who instructed Catherine had told her that she had own guardian angel. The Catholic Church clearly teaches: "From its beginning until death, human life is surrounded by (angels') watchful care and intercession. …beside each believer stands an angel as protector and shepherd leading him to life."[69] Dreadful things sometimes happen to people; and bring fear concerning their unknown outcomes. Loved ones can be terribly worried and distressed. Reliance on guardian angels is very much a part of Catholic belief. One's angel is present to prompt—though not force—what is good, and may very well enfold a person of faith protectively even in the worst kind of terror.

Photo by E. Sherman; cross by Fr. John Odermann, Valley City, ND

This is a rustic, though well-crafted crucifix,
the type of which brought tears to Catherine, thinking of how much her Savior had suffered.

---

68 Fr. Cholenec, *Positio* Document X, 1692, p. 257.

69 *Catechism of the Catholic Church*, #336

Chapter Seven: Catherine Dedicated Her Virginity to Jesus Christ.

As we have seen, even when she was quite young Catherine wished to remain unmarried.[70] As the years went on, and she got to know Jesus Christ, she chose that way of living out her love for Him. Another way to describe this is that she did not want to accept the status of being an earthly spouse, but rather that she chose to develop an intense relationship with Our Lord. For her, this meant being spouse to her Divine Love, Jesus Christ. Father Cholenec writes:

> *It was this burning love which made her renounce marriage to consecrate her virginity to Our Lord at the age of twenty* [Fr. Cholenec clarifies this in his 1715 writing, saying that she made the public vow of virginity at nearly age twenty-three.]*; and although she suffered many rough attacks from her kindred …, …, she held firm always with an unshakable constancy—surely a very admirable thing…. Catherine, who had a regard only for the things of heaven, thought herself happy to be able to lack everything and to be abandoned by everyone in order to be entirely consecrated to her Divine Spouse.*[71]

The freedom to accept the calling to be a virgin is just what Jesus spoke of when he said: "Some are incapable of marriage because they were born so; some, because they were made so by others; some, because they have renounced marriage for the sake of the kingdom of heaven. Whoever can accept this ought to accept it" (The Gospel according to Matthew, 19:12, NAB).

Catherine considered many things as she made the choice to continue unmarried. The life of a wife and mother would have appealed to her. Even her fervor as a Christian brought the need to clarify matters before she could be sure. Her main instructress, Anastasia, was apparently under the impression that a good Christian really ought to marry.

---

[70] Fr. Cholenec, *Positio* Document X, 1696, p. 243.

[71] Fr. Cholenec's part in *Positio* Document III, 1682, p. 82.

Courtesy of Kateri Shrine, Fonda, NY; photo by E. Sherman of their statue of Catherine

Father Cholenec writes:

Catherine… had come to him [Father Frémin[72]], *and opening her heart had asked him if it would be absolutely necessary for her to marry in order to be a good Christian, for so she had been told by her instructress. The priest explained the different states of life, telling her that God has left us free to marry or not,…. This filled her with joy, and she decided no longer to question the state of life which God had planned for her.*[73]

To say that Catherine claimed Jesus as her "spouse" means her love for Him can be called "spousal love." A spousal love is of the spirit, but it is also one of body as well as of soul. Some who are called by Christ to a spousal relationship with Him may thereby be called to virginity, and want their body and their soul to be kept special for Christ. Although different from the love that married people so rightly and holily may share, the love that a consecrated virgin shares with Christ can be equally warm and deep, and perhaps even more profound. Catherine for this reason would not marry; she reserved her spousal love for Christ alone.

This illustrates a wonderful truth. Each and every person is respected and loved by God, who foresees what is the holiest and happiest life that person can live. There is a special path for everyone. Though Jesus is truly God and has God the Father's special love, everyone else has that love too. It is good to meditate on Our Lord's experience at His own baptism: how God the Father claimed Him as His own beloved One. (cf. Mark 1:11). As special children through Baptism, each person is beloved by God.

---

[72] Father Jacques Frémin was the main authority (the superior) of the Sault Mission at the time. Later a Father Chomonot became superior.

[73] Fr. Chauchetière, *Op.Cit.*, pp 176-177.

Courtesy of Leona Gonzales

This is a little corn-husk doll, made in the traditional Mohawk way. Catherine had such as a child herself, and almost surely later made some for the children in her village, passing on loving and spiritual thoughts.

It is well known that Native people hold that their elders deserve special respect. Catherine respected her elders, even waiting some years to ask for Baptism, perhaps because her elders did not want her to. But when she realized that God willed otherwise, she chose what she was convinced God wanted. She chose to be baptized and also to be a virgin, and she lived up to all her promises.

Father Cholenec writes how Catherine's adopted sister approached her, urged her to marry, and said:

"You are of a marriageable age, and you need it,....."

The priest goes further and writes:

Catherine was strangely surprised by her sister's discourse, which she had not anticipated; but because she was very honest and had great respect for her sister, she did not show the pain which this caused her. She even thanked her for her good advice, and added that as the affair was of such great importance she wished to think it over at leisure. Our courageous virgin …sought me …to tell me the whole affair. "Catherine," I then said to her, "you are the judge in this matter. It depends on you alone; but think well, for it is a concern of great moment." She replied immediately, and without hesitation "Ah, my Father, I will not marry…....." In order to sound and test her more, I dwelt on the strong reasons which her sister had presented to her. She assured me with great firmness that the thought of poverty did not frighten her, that her work would always furnish her with what she needed to eat, and that a few rags would be enough to cover her. Then I sent her back assured that she was doing right.

Courtesy of Theresa Steele :Terrykateri@aol.com

A depiction by Algonquin Theresa Steele which represents Catherine in clothes given her by others.

Even the good Christian teacher, Anastasia, urged her to marry. About this, Father Cholenec continues:

Anastasia,…who was a wise woman…, fear(ing)…Catherine had taken this resolution lightly…did all in her power to change her decision, but she did not succeed any more than the other. Because she urged her so insistently, Catherine replied in a voice…more than usually firm, ….[74]

Courtesy of St. Francis Xavier Church/Museum, Kahnawake Reserve, Canada

This is like the representations of the cross such as one Catherine made by a river bank during the long stay in the forest when she helped on the winter hunt (Cf. Fr. Cholenec, *Positio* Document X, p.257, as quoted earlier.) [St. Francis Xavier's, where this picture is displayed, is at P.O. Box 70, Kahnawake, Qc J0L 1B0, with telephone (450) 632-6030]

[74] Fr. Cholenec, *Positio* Document .X, 1696, pp. 275-278.

Catherine, knowing the hardship her virginity could bring, nevertheless gave over to her heavenly Spouse the spiritual and bodily sufferings she endured, and which she willingly, voluntarily, and eagerly would undertake.

Catherine's life, with all her sufferings, from a worldly standpoint, might have seemed a waste. Yet people began to accept her choice, and she was a continual help to them. Father Cholenec writes:

The fruit of all this was that they no longer talked of anything but of being converted and of giving themselves entirely to God.[75]

Catherine, as the days went by, showed her love for her people, serving them, and suffering for them. We quote Father Chauchetière again:

Although she was infirm, she was always the first to be at work.[76]

Father Cholenec writes of the blessing she was for her people:

(Catherine) was by nature gentle, honest, affectionate, ..., kind, and always ready to lend a helping hand. Her patience in the midst of her continual suffering at the Sault appeared heroic to us; she bore it with a constancy and evenness of disposition that delighted us, ..., always contented, without ever manifesting impatience or the least sign of annoyance or sadness except the one time that her sister urged her marriage with such insistence.[77]

Many Native people see the acceptance of sufferings as an expression of thanks for being spared a harsh event, or for some good fortune that comes to them. They, and also some non-Native people, endure sufferings—even embrace them—for other peoples' needs. Sufferings, then, are seen as ways of "going beyond self," for the needs of the community. Every day of her life Catherine accepted sufferings.

---

[75] Fr. Cholenec's words, *Positio* Document III, 1682, pp. 86-87.

[76] Fr. Chauchetière, *Op.Cit.,*, p. 124:

[77] Fr. Cholenec, *Positio* Document X, 1696, pp, 296-297. [That outburst was toward Anastasia.]

Photo by E. Sherman of Station of the Cross # 7 at St. Michael's Church, Grand Forks, ND

From the earliest days Christians have traveled to places where Jesus suffered, or made representations for their pondering.

Catherine was convinced that suffering had great value for her own sake and for others. She often ate very little, or added bad-tastes to what she did eat. She accepted thorn-like wounds, and even asked that they be inflicted. Knowing the horror of burns done to captives (slaves), she even did that to herself, feeling this was giving deference to Our Lord.[78] When Anastasia instructed Catherine, she seems to have encouraged her to embrace sufferings.[79] Being told of this, the priests counseled moderation. Father Chauchetière wrote how she nevertheless persisted in her efforts.

> Catherine disclosed the sentiments of her heart in these words: "My Jesus, I must suffer for Thee; I love Thee, but I have offended Thee. …. I am very affected by the three nails which fastened Our Lord to the cross; they are but a symbol of my sins." … … A year passed in this manner, the year that Father Frémin spent in France. Perhaps his absence was the reason why they never spoke of what they were doing. Catherine fell ill and was in danger of death. It was then that her companion [that is, Marie-Thérèse] began to have scruples about letting Catherine die without telling anyone of their mortifications. Father Chomonot had charge of the mission …and it was to him that she went with the ready consent of the sick girl. The priest was greatly surprised; but without showing his astonishment, he reprimanded them for their indiscretion, which nevertheless he felt was pardonable in new Christians, and so he regulated their devotions. Catherine recovered, and … continually begged her confessor to permit her to do something, so that her body would not be the victor. He allowed her to do some things, but he restrained her, sometimes because … life … was already full of hardships. …. She did as much as she was permitted to do and asked permission in her last sickness to fast, because it was Holy Week. …. Catherine would answer … that Our Lord had been much more uncomfortable on the Cross and that she suffered nothing in comparison to Him.[80]

People suffer for their spouses or other loved ones. This is not saying that it would be good to tolerate a physically and/or psychologically abusive spouse. But in the normal give and take of married and family life, to love often means to suffer.

---

78 A *Positio* quote from Fr. Cholenec (Document X, 1696, pp. 288-289) gives his view about these self-inflicted sufferings: "to be admired, but not (necessarily) imitated." Father's words are not unique among wise spiritual advisers.

79 K.I. Koppedrayer, "The Making of the First Iroquois Virgin: Early Jesuit Biographies of the Blessed Kateri Tekakwitha," *Ethnohistory*, Spring 1993, p. 287; see also Fr. Cholenec, *Positio* Document XII, p. 373.

80 Fr. Chauchetière , *Op.Cit.*, pp. 184-186.

Photo by E. Sherman at Holy Family Church, Tuscarora Reservation, New York

This touching, but very thought-provoking statue group, is of Jesus, Mary, and Joseph. It can represent the holiness of marriage and family, with their loving sacrifices. It can also portray virginity, with its sacrifices done for love of others.

Both single and married life can be holy. The Catechism of the Catholic Church (#1629) quotes St. John Chrysostom: *"Whoever denigrates marriage also diminishes the glory of virginity. Whoever praises it makes virginity more admirable and resplendent. ..."*

The Catechism of the Catholic Church (#1617) says that the spousal relationship with Christ extends to the whole Church. Because of the passion, death, and resurrection of Jesus, each baptized person has been given, or at least offered, infinite Love. Virgins live principally for Christ, while interceding for all others; truly enlightened married people know their primary love is also for Christ, while holding no love back from their respective spouses. Nonetheless the Church believes there is something special about the relationship with Christ which a person acquires who chooses virginity for Him.[81]

Married persons are concerned about their spouses, while the virgin is free to be concerned about all the things of the Lord (cf. 1 Corinthians 7:32-34).

Both in marriage and in virginity, there can be beauty and closeness with God, and these two states of life help each other. The lives of those called to virginity can remind all others that the fullness of love is that of God. The lives of married people—in their lives together—can exemplify that same holy love.[82]

---

[81] Cf. Vatican II Decree regarding Religious Life, October 28, 1965, paragraph 12.

[82] Cf. *Virginity*, by Raniero Cantalamessa, Alba House, New York, 1995, pp. 63-64.

Photo by E. Sherman

George Ryder rings the bells each day at St. Francis Xavier Church, Kahnawake.
The participation of parishioners there is a great encouragement.

The virgin Catherine helped married people in their spiritual pursuits, as Father Chauchetière writes:

Two married persons called on Catherine shortly after she had embraced the state of perpetual virginity,…, with the purpose of learning from her the kind of life a good Christian should lead in this world.[83]

---

[83] Fr. Chauchetière, *Op. Cit.*, pp. 189-190.

Catherine's whole life was a help to her people. In earlier times, it seems that the Iroquois respected marriage very much, but increasingly alcohol introduced by Europeans brought harm to such stable unions.[84] Catherine wanted people to have nothing to do with alcohol. She urged her beloved friend Marie-Thérèse not to fall back into such wrong-doing.[85]

Photo by E. Sherman of painting at St. Francis Xavier Church/ Museum, Kahnawake Reverse, Canada

This painting of Catherine by Father Chauchetière, done just a few years after her death, shows her clothed in handed-down clothing.

Her sister wanted her to marry in order to have clothing and food, but Catherine did not worry, for she wanted to live poor for the good of her spirit. Father Cholenec tells us what she said to her sister:

---

84 *Ibid.*, p. 194.

85 *Ibid.*, p. 204. Early in this text there is a quote from that conversation—Catherine promising to help by prayer.

Catherine's answer was in a few words: that she was not afraid of the devil's snares, because she had trust in God alone; that she was unafraid of the scoffing men, for she had hopes she would do nothing but what was worthy of praise; and that as for her bodily necessities, she would find food by working for it, as no matter how little she might have, so much would always be enough.[86]

Religiously motivated virginity can enable one to know Jesus Christ in a very deep way, and even reflect the holiness and goodness of the Savior. The Catholic Church with its high regard for virgins, sees it as an honor to designate Catherine simply as "Virgin." But she can be extolled also for her willingness to be poor. Karol Wojtyla, better known as Pope John Paul II, writing about marriage and virginity, said: "...the Council seems to lay special stress on the value of poverty...."[87] (He is referring to the Second Vatican Council's *Constitution on the Church*, #42). Wanting—and even being eager—to live poorly fits well with consecrated virginity, for Jesus was both virgin and poor.

Knowing too, that Jesus gathers in love all who have belonged to Him, might it be that Catherine felt not only close to Him, but also even to her mother, whom she had missed so much from her very early years?

Hearing or reading what Catherine suffered should not be taken as a call for everyone to try to do what she did, but to imitate the love that was present in all she experienced. As Jesus accepted suffering to show His love for everyone, she did too.

But before she made a decision as unusual as the choosing of virginity—and the poverty that would go with it—Father Cholenec asked Catherine to wait. He wanted her to once more carefully consider what she was doing. He writes about how Catherine quickly came back to him with her answer:

"It is settled," said she, as she came near me; "it is not a question of deliberation; my part has long since been taken. No, my Father I can have no other spouse but Jesus Christ." I thought that it would be wrong for me any longer to oppose a resolution which seemed to me inspired by the Holy Spirit, and therefore exhorted her to perseverance, assuring her that I would take her part against those who

---

[86] Fr. Cholenec *Positio* Document XIII, 1715, pp. 394-5.

[87] *Sources of Renewal,"The Implementation of Vatican II" Harper & Row, San Francisco,1980 ,* p 194

wished henceforth to disturb her on that subject. This answer restored her former ranquillity of mind, and re-established in her soul that inward peace which she preserved even to the end of her life.[88]

Photo by E. Sherman

This tabernacle with Jesus in the Blessed Sacrament is at Seven Dolors on the Spirit Lake Reservation in North Dakota. Catherine is rightly pictured there, for she went again and again to church, knowing that Jesus was present, and longing all the more for the times when she could receive Him in Holy Communion.

With peace, Catherine gave herself spiritually to Christ. Father Cholenec wrote about the promise Catherine made to her Lord:

It was the Feast of the Annunciation,[89] March 25, 1679, at eight o'clock in the morning when, a moment after Jesus Christ gave Himself to her in Communion, Catherine Tegakoüita wholly gave herself to Him, and renouncing marriage forever, promised Him perpetual virginity. With a heart aglow

---

[88] Fr. Cholenec, *Positio* Document XII, 1715, p. 366.

[89] The Annunciation feast (named for the moment Archangel Gabriel announced to the Blessed Virgin Mary that God wished her to become the mother of Jesus) is fittingly observed each year exactly nine months before Jesus' birthday, December 25.

with love she implored Him to be her only Spouse, and to accept her as His bride. She prayed Our Lady, for whom she had a tender devotion, to present her to her Divine Son; then, wishing to make a double consecration in one single act, she offered herself entirely to Mary at the same time that she dedicated herself to Jesus Christ, earnestly begging her to be her mother and to accept her as her daughter. [90]

A little later this promised dedication did not diminish, but rather intensified. Father Cholenec writes:

…, in… love and gratitude for Jesus immolated on our altars and on the cross, and prompted by an intense desire to give all for all, after preparing herself by new devotions, she made, in Holy Communion, a perpetual offering of her soul to Jesus in the Holy Eucharist, and of her body to Jesus Crucified, taking Him again for her only Spouse, and devoting herself wholly to Him as bride. She chose a great feast of Our Lady[91] for this act, so as to make her offering to the Son through the hands of His divine Mother, and also in order to take her once more for her own. I may say that after she made these two great sacrifices of her soul and body, her soul lived only for Jesus in the Holy Eucharist, and her body lived only so as to die with Him on the Cross, in the midst of sorrow and suffering. I say die on the cross since she truly died on it, having shortened her days by an act worthy of eternal commemoration, although it is rather to be admired than imitated,….[92]

Hopefully no one should feel that virginity is fine only for people like Catherine. Though she and others are virgins their whole lives, everyone is called to be chaste and pure, and this means some times of "virginity"—that is, abstinence from sexual activity. The help of God, and the prayers of the Blessed Virgin Mary, make this possible. Physical sexual activity is right only for people who are married to each other in a holy union. And this purity brings God's blessings, which are happiness in heaven, but also happiness in this world.

The Bible's Old Testament has: *(Who) has…(God) so close to (them) as the LORD, our God, is to us whenever we call upon Him?* (Deuteronomy 4:7).

---

[90] Fr. Cholenec, *Positio* Document X, 1696, pp. 288-289.

[91] This could have been December 8, 1679, the Feast of the Immaculate Conception of Mary. That feast—not like that of March 25th, when Jesus' conception is remember and He began to live in Mary's womb—is in remembrance of Mary's holy beginning in *her* mother's womb.

[92] Fr. Cholenec, *Positio* Document X, 1696, p. 294.

God's desire for closeness is shown in all Catherine's experiences. She guarded against dangerous situations that could lead to impurity, and would certainly have confessed the slightest—even initial—activity endangering purity. Father Chauchetière writes: *Catherine ... overcame the greatest demon ... of impurity, a sin the very shadow of which made her afraid, and as she was always careful to flee the occasion of it, she had no trouble in avoiding it;*[93]

Catherine was not alone in the determination to live purely. There were many temptations to do unchaste things in those days, as of course, there are today. Her peoples' trips to the trade-center of Montreal, for example, could mean great danger in this regard. Father Cholenec tells how two Christian Indian men, perhaps by Catherine's example, saw the need for vigilance during a busy time there:

> (They) *assembled the girls and women in a place apart, and then guarded this camp all night, preventing the women from leaving or the men from entering it.*[94]

Courtesy of St Francis Xavier Church/Museum, Kahnawake Reserve, Canada

---

[93] Fr. Chauchetière, *Op.Cit.*, p. 139.

[94] Fr. Cholenec, *Positio* Document X, 1696, p. 285.

Catherine's own firm resolve to be chaste was seen and imitated by old and young alike. Father Chauchetière writes:

> Those …sanctify themselves by imitating Catherine, whose example they keep before them in living as good Christians. When they die the relation between their lives and that of Catherine will be evident. The men as well as the women take part in this imitation and several maidens have gone to heaven bearing the precious jewel of virginity.[95]

Referring to the influence for good that Catherine often had, the writer of this text remembers with gratitude the help that a girl gave to him years ago. With other dating boys and girls of his age, he had started to begin to get dangerously chummy with his date. Another girl in the group gave a glance his way, with clear disappointment in him for risking doing something wrong. That girl's goodness proved a deterrent, a helping grace to be more determined to choose God's way, and the closeness that God offers.

In the following passage Father Cholenec gives us additional insight into the closeness Catherine had with Our Lord in her life and in her prayers:

> To keep alive her devotion for the mystery of Our Savior's Passion, and to have it always present to her mind, she carried on her breast a little crucifix which I had given her. She often kissed it with feelings of the most tender compassion for the suffering Jesus, and with the most vivid remembrance of the benefits of our redemption.[96]

---

95 Fr. Chauchetière, *Op.Cit.*, p. 118.

96 Fr. Cholenec, *Positio* Document XII, 1715, page 372.

Courtesy of Pope John Paul II Cultural Center, Washington, DC

> On an earlier picture St. Thérèse's, words were shown: "I will spend my time in heaven doing good on earth."
> Catherine said very much the same thing just before she died: "I will love you in heaven. I will help you. I will pray for you."

Father Cholenec goes on to relate how Catherine had special help from God to go beyond words in her prayer life. Her way of praying—that is, by seeming to be simply "looking at Jesus"—is often called "mystical prayer." He writes:

She made the Lord Jesus hidden in the Sacrament of the Altar her one exercise of devotion, her one source of nourishment and encouragement. …once she was shown the excellence and dignity of that great mystery,…she glowed with love of Him! … before sunrise, even in the coldest depth of winter, Catherine would be found in prayer at the church door; nor would she go home before she had heard all the Masses. With similar zeal she was the first at the evening prayers in the church, and when the others had gone, she stayed longer to pray. She was quite motionless at prayer. She prayed little with the lips, much from the heart, not merely with attention, but in some wonderful way inflamed. You would surely have said she was not so much believing in the hidden Jesus as looking at Him there present. At times even her face was aglow with beams, as it were, from the flame within.[97]

---

97 Fr. Cholenec, *Positio* Document XIII, 1715, p. 390.

Chapter Eight: Catherine Has Her last Days Full Of Holiness

Even when Catherine was very ill, she sometimes had to stay completely alone in her cabin. The work of Native people was relentless, as they planted or harvested, and did the many tasks their very existence demanded. She was glad for this time to pray. But it soon became plain that Catherine could not live much longer. her closest friends wanted to stay near, but she told them not to worry, seeming to know the day, and perhaps even the hour, when her death would come. She assured them they could come back in time. Father Cholenec writes of those days and hours:

> As the time of her last moments approached, her strength was constantly decreasing until the beginning of Holy Week, 1680, … . Tuesday morning, seeing that she was sinking rapidly, we gave her the Holy Viaticum, … . The Divine Savior was no sooner with her than she renewed all the offerings she had made Him, … .   All of our Indians who were at the village, and who had accompanied the Blessed Sacrament to the lodge, were charmed by such edifying piety. She passed the remainder of that day and the following night in sweet and fervent communion with Our Lord, Our Lady, and her crucifix. Wednesday morning she received Extreme Unction with the same devotion with which she had received the Holy Viaticum on the preceding day. …A little later she lost her power of speech while pronouncing the holy names of Jesus and Mary, but … her hearing was still very good and she was fully conscious until her last breath, … . (In) a short half hour … she died peacefully, as if she had entered into a light sleep.[98]

Both of the sacraments, in the words used for them during Catherine's times, are very much valued in our time as well. However, "Extreme Unction" — which means 'the very last anointing' — is more recently called the "Anointing of the Sick." It is now given not just when death is near, but for help during the time of illness. Holy Communion is brought to the sick as well, and when death *is* near, this gift of Our Lord brings Him to be their companion into the next world. Holy Communion at that time is called "Viaticum," meaning 'with you on your journey.'

---

98 Fr. Cholenec, *Positio* Document X, 1696, p.302.

Photo by E. Sherman; Kateri gift shop, National Shrine of N. American Martyrs, Auriesville, NY

Catherine's last hours were moving ones for all her fellow Kahnawake neighbors, as they prayed with her. She received Viaticum (Holy Communion) and Extreme Unction (now called Anointing of the Sick).

For peoples in all centuries, the end of earthly life comes all too frequently for those they know and love. This was perhaps especially true for Native people. They had beliefs about what followed death; that there is a future life they had no doubt. Many, however, believed the soul of the departed would linger near for some days, and then, after the mourning of loved ones, it could proceed and travel along the Milky Way, the Path of Souls. A special remembrance would follow one year later.[99]

Courtesy of Fordham University Press, from their *Positio*. Permission received.

Catherine (Kateri) died on April 17, 1680.
Everyone present remembered her death as beautiful, including what happened moments later.

Kahnawake residents witnessed how Catherine had lived and was now passing from earthly life. What they saw reassured them that death could be full of promise, with Jesus Christ present at the end, as well as all through life.

---

99 Snow, *Op. Cit.,* p.104. (The wording in the text above is in the past tense, yet for not a few, some similar outlooks—or some very dissimilar ones—are held at the present time.)

Jesus Christ came from heaven, for He is God. He has gone back—that is, ascended—to heaven. He said: "*Do not let your hearts be troubled. You have faith in God; have faith also in me. In my Father's house, there are many dwelling places. If there were not, would I have told you that I am going to prepare a place for you? And if I go and prepare a place for you, I will come back again and take you to myself, so that where I am you also may be.*"[100]

The reader may well have noticed that most of the portrayals of Catherine show her as beautiful—or at least unmarred—by the scars left from smallpox. That is the way many artists choose to present her, and it may be because people look forward to how things will be in heaven. Actually in life her face was terribly scarred. But something amazing happened for Catherine right on her deathbed, something that deeply affected those around her. After seeing her put herself completely into Jesus' hands and die, they witnessed a great sign of God's favor. Almost unbelievably her face changed. The scars cleared away, and she looked beautiful and wholly unmarked. It was one more sign that they had lived with a Saint, and that their beloved Catherine was now with her Divine Lover in heaven.

Chapter Seven: Catherine from Heaven Continues Her Good

In her earthly life, Catherine had intimacy with God. Catholic faith tells us that such an intimacy continues in heaven. Father Cholenec relates how Father Chauchetière later experienced a vision of Catherine in the happiness of heaven:

> *Having spoken until now of Catherine's life and death, we shall consider some apparitions that concern her, …. ….I admit that I have had difficulty in deciding whether to speak of it, for there are only too many people in the world who set themselves up to believe nothing, especially in matters of this kind. They no sooner hear apparitions mentioned than they protest against them and pretend these revelations are so many illusions and hallucinations,…. ….The apparitions I am referring to here are so important and clear in detail that I do not see how they could be reasonably called in question. Though the incredulous will always remain so, God will be no less glorified in His Servant, and virtuous people*

---

100 The Gospel according to John, Chapter 14, verses 1-3. (NAB)

will find in these marvels new motives to love and bless Him, on seeing how liberal He is in rewarding the services rendered to Him, ….

The sixth day after Catherine's death, that is to say, the Monday after Easter, a person of virtue and worthy of belief was praying at four o'clock in the morning, [this was Father Chauchetière[101]] *when Catherine appeared to him surrounded by glory, with majestic bearing and shining face lifted toward heaven as if in ecstasy,…wishing by so marked a favor to acknowledge the great service she had received from him during her lifetime.*[102]

Photo by E. Sherman

This is the tomb-site where Catherine was first buried. It is along the St. Lawrence River, just down stream from Kahnawake.

---

101 This insertion is by E. Sherman. Father Chauchetière clearly is the one Catherine made this visitation to, giving instructions about her wishes, including the paintings he would do.

102 Fr. Cholenec, *Positio* Document X, 1696, pp. 311-312.

The cross is not separated from a holy life. Another appearance of Catherine—this time to Anastasia— made it clear how the cross can bring glory. Many pictures and statues of Catherine are correct in showing her with a cross, holding it high. She loved the cross of Jesus, and she herself never ran from sufferings. Rather, she embraced those difficult moments with intense love for Christ. This is Father Cholenec relates:

Catherine (also) appeared to the good Anastasia…. This fervent Christian woman …(was)… in prayer… after the others of her lodge had gone to bed. … she finally lay down on her mat to rest, but …she was awakened by a voice which called her with these words: "Mother, arise." She recognized Catherine's voice. Far from having any fear…, turning to the place whence the voice came, she saw Catherine standing beside her, brilliant with light. …. She carried a cross in her hand which was more brilliant than everything else, …. "I saw her," she insisted, "…(and) heard these words very distinctly: 'Mother, look at this cross and see how beautiful it is. It was the source of all my happiness during my life, and I counsel you to make it yours also.'" After these few words she disappeared, leaving her mother overjoyed and with a spirit so filled with this vision that after many years her memory of it is as fresh as it was the first day.[103]

Catherine followed the way that she was convinced God called her to live, and she did so with the help of God's grace and the prayers of the mother of Jesus. Her love for Mary is clearly recorded; for example, she showed her reliance on that mother through the rosary. She kept a rosary close to her, and prayed it regularly. We have the words of Father Cholenec for this:

What can be thought after this, except to say with the prophet that God is admirable in His Saints (Ps. 67:36), and that, having chosen this one …, …He had protected her by His blessings, so to speak, from the moment she left her mother's womb. From this source resulted her tender affection for Our Lady, the Queen of Virgins, and the Mother of purity. As soon as Catherine learned about her she loved her ecstatically, and spoke of her with enthusiasm. She learned by heart the litanies composed in her honor, and said them every evening in private after the common prayers of the lodge. She never went about without her beads, which she recited in all her goings and comings.[104]

---

103 Ibid., p. 314.

104 *Ibid.*, p. 298.

Photo by E. Sherman, at St. Francis Xavier Church, Kahnawake Reserve, Canada

The community of Kahnawake became the home of her people not long after Catherine died. It was natural that a beautiful church be built there, and it is there today, St. Francis Xavier Church. Not far from its main altar and Blessed Sacrament tabernacle, on the east side of the church, is the place where her remains were moved. It is pictured above.
The church is open daily, and all visitors are welcome at this holy place.

Photo by E. Sherman at St. Francis Xavier Church, Kahnawake Reserve, Canada

This is the altar of St. Francis Xavier Church in Kahnawake, just feet away from the present tomb of Catherine. Mass is celebrated there regularly by a devoted Catholic priest pastor and faith-filled parishioners and very welcome pilgrim visitors.

Through the centuries, thousands have shown deep respect for Catherine, praying that she intercede with God in their behalf. Native and non-Native people look to her.[105] They gather together in groups such as the National Tekakwitha Conference, and in innumerable Kateri Circles. To hear about Catherine can increase the desire to know more about God, and inspire the listener to live a deeper spiritual life. Many have been helped because of her petitions to God for assistance.

---

[105] Contemporary mention of Catherine is found in writings other than those of the missionaries. Cf. Greer, *Op Cit.*, pp. 147-148.

Father Chauchetière, less than a year after Catherine's death, prayed to her to intercede with God in behalf of a dying man, and help came for him.[106] And such things have not stopped. Many today testify to blessings that have come through the prayers of this saintly woman.

Photo by E. Sherman, of a photo of and owned by Father G. McCarthy, Bisbee, ND

Mass and other prayers are part of many peoples' lives. The above is Mass during a "sobriety ride" sponsored by Turtle Mountain Chippewa and Spirit Lake Dakota Sioux in northeastern North Dakota. Riders support one another in their great quest for continued freedom especially from the affliction of alcohol. It was a concern of Catherine even in her day.

---

106 Fr. Cholenec, *Positio* Document X, 1696, pp. 316-317.

Most of all, this wonderful Native woman turns minds and hearts toward God. She did not see the possession of wealth as the great goal of life.

Eyewitnesses tell us that in the last moments before Catherine's death, she said: "Jesus, I love you!"[107]

The love of Jesus and the presence of the Holy Spirit gives the power to speak beautiful final words, and to know that the Savior is present to be one's company into heaven forever.

photo by E. Sherman, at the Pope John Paul II Cultural Center, Washington, DC

The late Pope John Paul II beatified (that is, gave the title "Blessed" to) Catherine "Kateri" Tekakwitha. He has said: "Look to her for an example of fidelity; see in her a model of purity and love; turn to her for assistance."

---

107 Fr. Chauchetière, *Op. Cit.*, p. 208.

Many today pray and yearn for the moment when the Catholic Church will officially bestow upon Catherine the title "Saint." For Catherine's canonization—as the bestowal of that title is called—there must occur a physical miracle which clearly is a result of her interceding with God for that favor.

Favors have come for sick people in their need. Loved ones had been asking Catherine to intercede with God for those peoples' physical recovery. God can give this recovery, and faith tells us that He will again. Though the writer of this text cannot claim to have seen such a complete and permanent physical recovery, he will always remember a number of occasions where there has been help, and the courage and peace the help has brought.

-One person, apparently feeling not worthy of God's love, suddenly asked for forgiveness. After receiving that, and then receiving that forgiveness, and then receiving Holy Communion, there followed moments of thoughtful and confident quiet, and a beautiful and sincere sign of the cross. Her physical health was not restored, but she received spiritual health that will last forever.

-Another, for whom many prayed for healing, was given years and years of almost unexpected earthly life. No one could be missed more than she, now that she is gone. But every bit of her life was a blessing to the multitude of people that knew her. And she herself is one whom her Lord and Catherine in heaven must have greeted: "Well done, good faithful servant!"

Continued prayers will lead to the recognition of Catherine as having always been deserving of being publicly called a saint. During all the years to come, those prayers will result in well-being for people everywhere. Her life is one to be admired, and in many ways imitated. Her loving closeness with Jesus Christ means everyone can turn to her for physical and spiritual good health.

Iroquois cornhusk doll

Courtesy of Leona Gonzales

Very likely Catherine adorned little corn-husk dolls such as pictured here.

Two years after Catherine's death, a well-documented spiritual healing was received. Any person who has suffered an addiction or other vice will appreciate the following:

Two persons were afflicted that way, and Catherine was asked to pray for them and seek Jesus' help. Those people received help, and got relief from those burdens as asked. Father Cholenec writes:

The Father went to this woman's cabin. The strange state in which he found her made him compassionate for her sufferings. He gave her Catherine's crucifix to place around her neck and had her begin a novena in her honor. This was the first novena made to her, and it was not without effect, for on the ninth day the woman was cured and has now for thirteen or fourteen years been without her sickness. Seeing that she had completely recovered, the Father told her to remember that she had promised Catherine not to gamble any more, of which she was inordinately fond. She gave it up entirely and has never gambled since.

(Another) man who was cured before her(,) spent five years in fighting a vice to which he was subject, and of which he promised Catherine to rid himself. It has been noticed that she usually cured the soul of those whose bodies she healed, if they were in need of this double assistance, even though they did not pray for it.[108]

Such instances are numerous. The missionaries recorded a variety of physical and spiritual miracles received when Catherine was asked to intercede with God.

The Church is thankful when favors of any kind are received, and will evaluate any that are submitted for study. In 2006, Monsignor Paul Lenz, until recently director of the Bureau of Catholic Indian Missions, became the acting vice-postulator for the cause for the canonization for Catherine "Kateri" Tekakwitha. He is a longtime promoter of this effort, and cares very much about Native and non-Native peoples. Monsignor Lenz has met and come to know very many people, for he has worked very hard for the missions. He is glad when spiritual favors brought about by Tekakwitha's intercession are received, and he will be overjoyed when a fairly recent physical cure from her is submitted and declared clearly miraculous. It will make possible her canonization, and the public recognition of her as *Saint* Catherine "Kateri" Tekakwitha. Monsignor Lenz wants to be told of your prayers for the intercession of Tekakwitha. When favors are received, write to him at 2021 H Street, NW, Washington, DC 20006-4207," or call (202) 331-8542.

---

108 Fr. Cholenec, *Positio* Document X, 1696, pp. 320.

Courtesy of Leona Gonzales

This corn-washing basket allows water to flow out, but leaves the corn intact, ready when needed. Catherine and her Native companions fashioned such helps with the skill of centuries of experience. It is pictured here because of its beauty, but an expertly-made work like this can encourage trust that prayer can bring cleansing. Holy Catherine wants each person to be the beautiful one that Jesus, with the Father and the Holy Spirit, has created and redeemed, washed in the Blood of the Lamb!

Everyone is invited to turn to Tekakwitha, asking her to beseech God for healings of themselves or someone else. The following is a good prayer:

"O God, who among the many marvels of Your Grace in the New World, did cause to blossom on the banks of the Mohawk, and of the St. Lawrence, the pure and tender Lily, Kateri Tekakwitha, grant we beseech You, the favor we beg through her intercession; that this Young Lover of Jesus and of His Cross may soon be counted among her Saints by Holy Mother Church, and that our hearts may be enkindled with a stronger desire to imitate her innocence and faith. Through the same Christ Our Lord. Amen."

(Bishop H. J. Hubbard of Albany, NY, approved the above prayer.)

Around 1685, just five years after she died, Father Chauchetière painted Catherine holding the cross she so often embraced as a devout follower of Jesus.[109] Though realistic in some ways, for in her poverty she likely often dressed in handed-down clothing, she is portrayed as almost between earth and heaven. This picture is in St. Francis Xavier Church on the Kahnawake Mohawk Reserve on the south bank of the St. Lawrence River across from Montreal. Her tomb is there, and a wonderful church and museum. Father Chauchetière's painting of Catherine is mid-way in this text, placed along side that of Saint Thérèse of Lisieux, and repeated later in a larger form.

There are many portrayals of Tekakwitha, some no doubt resembling her more than others. By study and prayer, anyone can get to know her, live more like her, and find the treasure she did: Jesus Christ.

---

109 Fr. Chauchetière, *Op. Cit.*, p. 115.

This book ends with a picture of a recently sculpted statue of Catherine Tekakwitha, in place in the Basilica of the National Shrine of the Immaculate Conception, Washington, DC. It portrays her holding high the cross, and cherishing the rosary. It shows how this holy woman lived constantly in union of the cross of Jesus Christ, and devoutly prayed the Blessed Virgin Mary's rosary.

photo by E. Sherman at the Basilica of the National Shrine of the Immaculate Conception, Washington, DC

Index [example: An item such as "n2" refers to a footnote on page 2.]